Holiday Walks in Tuscany

Norman Buckley

Copyright © 2003, Norman Buckley

Published by Sigma Leisure – an imprint of
Sigma Press, 5 Alton Road, Wilmslow, Cheshire SK9 5DY, England.

British Library Cataloguing in Publication Data
A CIP record for this book is available from the British Library.

ISBN: 1-85058-776-0

Typesetting and Design by: Sigma Press, Wilmslow, Cheshire.

Cover design by: Sigma Press

Printed by: Ashford Colour Press Ltd

Cover photographs: main picture, sunflowers near Certaldo (*Graham Beech*); smaller pictures, left to right, Chianti woodland (*Norman Buckley*), San Gimignano from the Gran Torre *(Graham Beech)*, Florence from the Boboli Gardens *(Norman Buckley)*

Text photographs: Norman and June Buckley

Maps: Bute Cartographics

DISCLAIMER

Preface

As a holiday destination for British visitors, Tuscany needs no introduction. For a variety of very good reasons – wine, climate, art, history and, by no means least, the delectable countryside, it has long attracted large numbers from these shores.

Indeed, Tuscany is so well loved that many have purchased properties of all shapes and sizes as holiday homes or, in some cases, as permanent residences in this seductive place.

This book puts the case for comparatively gentle country walking to be included as a very attractive part of the overall lure of Tuscany. As always in this series it is assumed that the non-Italian speaking walker will expect clear directions for finding the starting point and comprehensive route guidance for the complete circuit, together with background information which notes places of interest and refreshment possibilities. In other words, a reassuring feeling of certainty before undertaking any of the recommended walks.

To put this core requirement into the wider Tuscany context, further information has been included covering some of the relevant features, including those mentioned above, hopefully enhancing the enjoyment to be gained from walking through this lovely countryside.

Acknowledgements

Thanks to – my wife, June, whose support role always plays a vital part in our various walking enterprises, and to the staff of many tourist information offices, who supplied a wealth of useful information.

Free Internet Update Service

This book will be updated whenever it is reprinted, but be sure to check our website for updates and corrections in the meantime. This service is completely free of charge – just go to the "updates" section on our web site at: **www.sigmapress.co.uk**

We welcome your input to this service – if you encounter any problems on the walks or have any comments, please send your suggestions to us either by post (address on back cover) or by e-mail to: **info@sigmapress.co.uk**

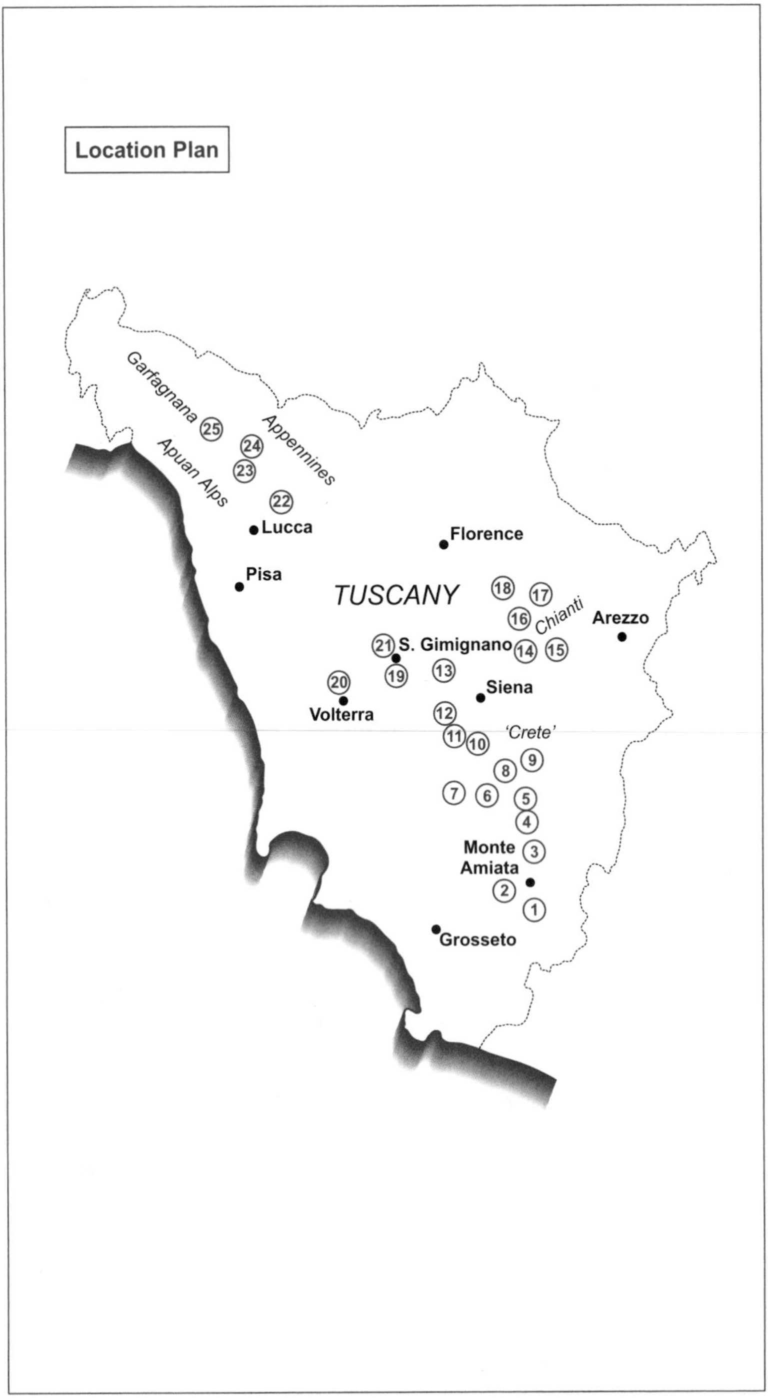

Location Plan

Garfagnana
Appennines
Apuan Alps

㉕25
㉔24
㉓23
㉒22

● Lucca
● Florence
● Pisa

TUSCANY

⑱18 ⑰17
⑯16 *Chianti*
● Arezzo

㉑21 ● S. Gimignano
⑭14 ⑮15
⑲19 ⑬13
● Siena

⑳20
Volterra

⑫12
⑪11 ⑩10 *'Crete'*
⑨9
⑧8
⑦7 ⑥6 ⑤5
④4

Monte ③3
Amiata ●
②2
①1

● Grosseto

Contents

Introducing Tuscany

THE WALKS

The South

South/Central

North/Central

The North

Introducing Tuscany

History

Not surprisingly in an area of such favourable climate and topography, Tuscany was settled by man as long ago as the Palaeolithic period, with gradual transition from hunter-gatherers to a Bronze Age 'Terramare' culture producing earth mounds and fortified settlements.

In more recent times and of much more importance to today's topography, from 1200 BC onwards there was southerly migration of various Indo-European peoples. From 900 BC the Etruscans arrived in much of Northern Italy, particularly Tuscany, to which they gave their name, becoming firmly established in a civilization based on twelve semi-independent city states. In addition to the development of internal trade throughout Europe, they were also a maritime people, competing with the Phoenicians, the Carthaginians and the Greeks for Mediterranean trade. By 800 BC the Etruscans were the dominating force in Italy, displaying their skills in architecture, engineering and art. They founded then ruled the city/state of Rome until expulsion in 510 BC, the date of the establishment of the Republic. The Etruscans were skilled builders and engineers but, apart from their extensive and elaborate necropolis areas (they had a very developed cult of the dead) there are comparatively few surviving structures, their towns and cities being overbuilt by later occupants, particularly the Romans.

Over the next few hundred years, as the Etruscans declined, the power of Rome grew enormously, with the conquest of central Italy completed by 280 BC. Although there were battles, much of the Roman take-over of the Etruscans in Tuscany was by absorption and a progressive Latinisation of the people.

For the next few hundred years, the history of Tuscany was the history of Rome, being part of the great empire as it ebbed and flowed, with civil wars and progressive expansion until its eventual decline and the fall of Rome itself to the Visigoths in AD 410. The Huns and the Vandals were involved in the confusing history of the ensuing centuries, with little stability, although a Lombard kingdom was established in Upper Italy for more than 200 years, until conquest by Charlemagne in AD 773-774.

The ensuing centuries saw conflict for power between German emperors and the Pope and the formation of two parties – the Ghibellines who supported the Emperor and the Guelfs who supported the Pope. The issue was confused by the emerging power and wealth of the city/states, initially localised but gradually expanding, and by the rise of powerful families such as the Medici. The city/states were generally aligned with the Pope, whilst surrounding territory was usually imperial.

In common with the whole of Italy, there was total fragmentation of government, with the power and influence of cities such as Florence, Siena, Pisa and Lucca producing prolonged conflicts and a great surge of castle building throughout the area. Remarkably, from about 1250 the immense flowering of the arts known as the Renaissance grew steadily around the focal points of the principal city/states as the rediscovery of ancient literature inspired the poetry and scholarship of many remarkable men.

From the middle of the 15th century, the German emperors had fought their last Italian campaigns, leaving something of a power vacuum which both France and Spain tried to fill, but without success. In 1569, one of the Medici family, the Duke of Florence, became established as the Grand Duke of Tuscany but, in 1737, Tuscany passed to the Emperor of Austria in compensation for the loss of Lorraine. The emperor ruled the grand duchy through a regent. This arrangement prevailed until the Napoleonic Wars, when Napoleon became King of Italy and his sister was appointed Grand Duchess of Tuscany.

After Napoleon's downfall, the former states were restored but there was now a strong tide for unification and for democracy running. In Tuscany the Grand Duke introduced some liberalization, but widespread revolution in 1848 brought about his downfall and flight, with the proclamation of a Republic. In 1860, a general revolution led by Garibaldi deposed the other princely rulers, unifying Italy. The following year, Victor Emmanuel II became the first King of Italy, with Florence as capital city, later changed to Rome.

In the 20th century, the first World War, the rise of fascism under Mussolini, the alliance with Hitler in World War II, the downfall of fascism and the change of sides in 1943 followed by the abdication of King Victor Emmanuel III and the creation of a republic in 1946, have left Italy as a modern democratic country, and a prominent member of the European Community

Art

The Etruscans left large numbers of urns, fragments of gateways and necropoli which demonstrate their architectural and artistic abilities. By way of contrast, in artistic terms Roman remnants are less impressive, although walls, amphitheatres and the theatre at

Volterra do remain. The most important centre for Roman monuments is Fiesole, close to Florence.

Despite the interest of these ancient remains, the overwhelming artistic achievements in Tuscany took place during the 14th to 16th centuries – the 'Renaissance' – that period of the rebirth of the spirit of antiquity, which brought forth a great flowering of poetry, literature, architecture, sculpture and painting, an unprecedented outpouring of work of matchless quality. The great cities of Tuscany led the world in this movement, building huge and beautiful cathedrals and palaces – Florence, Siena, Pisa, Lucca and others – and scores of lesser churches and palaces, many of them equally beautiful, whilst the sculptors and painters produced huge numbers of masterpieces, primarily of religious subjects.

Florence soon became, and has since remained, the Christian art capital of the world, with the Uffizzi gallery and its collection as the focal point.

A walks book is not the place to list the hundreds of names of those who contributed to the glory of this period or to attempt any detailed analysis, but no visitor can be unaware of its importance to the overall appreciation of Tuscany and to the enjoyment of the landscape in its widest context.

Landscape

Woodland, vineyards, olive groves and arable fields are the essential ingredients of the much admired classic Tuscan landscape. In the Garfagnana, to the north, the long valley of the Serchio, bounded by the mighty peaks of the Apuan Alps and the Appennines, provides a very different landscape and a different type of walking, particularly for those who go high on the moun-

Springtime countryside at Volpaia (Walk 16)

tains. Likewise the region of Monte Amiata in the south is different, the great bulk of the wooded former volcano defining the landscape of a wide area, not least in the proliferation of warm springs and the consequent emergence of spa towns and villages such as Bagno Vignoni, Sarteano and Bagni San Filippo.

Although the classic Tuscan landscape is spacious, it is unusual to be out of sight of the evidence of human modification of that landscape in the shape of buildings great and small, particularly as the builders, from medieval times, sited their farms, their castles, their churches, their towns and villages and ultimately their cities on the tops of hills whenever possible, becoming highly visible focal features in the rolling countryside. Fortunately, the vast majority of these constructions have been constructed in sympathetic local materials, the ochre walls and the shapely spires and towers now greatly adding to our overall appreciation and to the interest of our walks.

Industry

There is a long history of extractive industries in this part of Italy. Mineral ores such as iron, copper, lead, zinc, mercury and antimony have long been mined around Monte Amiata and in the 'Metalliferous Hills' south-west of Siena. There was also coal mining in the area south of Murlo. Most of the mines and their associated furnaces are now closed.

Most significant is the marble quarrying in the Apuan Alps, with its immense effect on the landscape. White Carrera marble, inspiration of Michaelangelo and many others, has been world-famous for centuries.

Along the valley of the Arno, to the west of Florence, and part of the adjacent valley of the Elsa, textile and other factories contribute to Tuscany's most industrial landscape. In the Metaliferous Hills, the exploitation of geo-thermal energy has resulted in the construction of a large power station at Larderello.

Wine

To say that the growing of vines and the production of wine is important in Tuscany is a gross understatement. From at least Etruscan times it has been a major element of cultivated land use; in more recent centuries it has also been of great economic importance.

However, until comparatively recently it would have been true to say that with a few notable exceptions quantity generally prevailed over quality, as the absence of any imposed or recognised standards left producers free to maximise output by whatever means. After neighbouring France introduced its *Appellation Controlle* quality controls in the 1930s, attempts were made to bring order into the situation; unfortunately these were curtailed by World War II. In the late 1960s laws providing for *'Denominazione di Origine Controllata'* were introduced, prescribing limits on the yields per hectare together with other quality requirements, but some uncertainty still remained. In 1992 the law was tightened, with the introduction of a new DOCG (wines of controlled and guaranteed designation of origin) standard. It should be mentioned that, until the 1960s a high proportion of agriculture in Tuscany was subject to the historic system of semi-tenure, whereby half the yield went to the landowner (*padrone*), with the peasant farmers (*contadini*) retaining the other half. The termination of this system by economic necessity brought about a considerable social revolution which resulted in the sale and amalgamation of many small vineyards, facilitating the introduction of modern, more business-like methods and proper control of the output. The peasant economy and the centuries of concomitant peasant society were speedily swept aside. Whilst quality was for so long being widely neglected, two 19th-century pioneers of wine improvement are worthy of note. Baron Ricosoli of Brolio Castle, a member of a noble family owning vast estates from medieval times to the present day and the Santi family in the Montalcino area both experimented with the prevailing Sangiovese grape and its improvement as the strict basis for the best Chianti and other red wines.

The climate of Tuscany is mild Mediterranean, with shelter from ranges of mountains contributing to very favourable wine-growing conditions. The average quality of the wine is considerably higher than that for Italy as a whole.

Finally, mention must be made of Vino Santo, sweet, strong nectar made from dried grapes, traditionally produced in small quantities by peasant farmers then stored in wooden casks for up to 10 years. This

The Chianti Classico cockerel sculpture at Greve (Walk 18)

wine was kept for use on high days and holidays and as an offering to special guests. Today's Vino Santo is obviously produced on a commercial basis, but quantities are still comparatively small, with correspondingly high prices.

Consistent with the local lifestyle, visitors to Tuscany can obviously enjoy a wide variety of good wines at very modest cost, either purchased at the vineyards or the grocery shop, sampled in the specialist 'Enoteca' bars or enhancing a meal at café or restaurant. In the latter case, even the modest house wine will rarely disappoint.

Travelling to Tuscany

Air

By air is probably the favourite method of travelling from the United Kingdom to all destinations in Italy. For Tuscany, the international airport at Pisa, with frequent direct flights from many airports in Britain, is the most convenient. There are good road and rail connections to other centres such as Florence and Lucca. For Siena, the road is good but by rail is less convenient, a change at Empoli to a minor line being required.

For destinations in the north-east of Tuscany there is an airport at Bologna, for the south some might prefer to use Rome airport. There is a minor airport at Florence which has a very limited range of direct flights to and from Britain.

Rail

In recent years the speed and convenience of long distance rail services across France to Italy and other countries has been greatly improved. Use of Eurostar from London, followed by French TGV and similar Italian high-speed services, can now be thoroughly recommended. With a change at Paris, and possibly also at Milan, the time to Florence is a little over 17 hours (overnight).

Car

Many visitors, perhaps for reasons of economy, quantity of luggage and/or preference for one's own familiar vehicle, will prefer to undertake the drive across France. Tuscany can be reached in two long days from, say, the Midlands, using the excellent motorway systems. Several permutations of route are possible, the choice being very subjective, taking into account such factors as the cost of tolls and a tolerance or otherwise of long Alpine tunnels. One way or another, there are high mountain barriers to be crossed. One recommended route is to cross France from Calais (ferry or the shuttle through the tunnel) – A26 – St Quentin – Reims – Troyes – A5 – A31 – Dijon – A39 – Bourg en Bresse – A40 – Nantua – Geneva – Mont Blanc Tunnel (refurbished after closure for several years – 25 Euro toll charge) – Aosta – A5 – A4 – A26 – A10 – Genoa. For various destinations in Tuscany, use A11, A12 or A15 onwards. This is probably the most direct route generally, but for eastern Tuscany crossing part of Switzerland and crossing the Alps by the St Gothard route might be preferred. (In this case, don't forget the cost of purchasing a Swiss motorway pass.)

Motorail

A compromise, in that one has the use of one's own car in Tuscany, with the advantage of luggage capacity and familiarity, but avoiding the long drive through France and the crossing of the Alps. In summer, there are overnight services from Calais to Nice and from Brussels to Milan, but in winter reduced services operate only from Lille to Nice or from Brussels to Milan. From Nice the A8 then A10 motorways run behind the French and Italian Riviera to reach Tuscany. In all cases Motorail is comparatively expensive but the difference is obviously reduced when petrol, motorway tolls and overnight stop costs are brought into the equation.

Rail Europe Travel Centre, 178, Piccadilly, London W1 (08705 848 848). Other relevant agencies can be found on the Internet, including *euro destination.com*.

Travelling within Tuscany

Rail

Main railway lines connect Florence with the cities of the north and east, such as Milan, Turin, Bologna and Venice, and with Rome to the south. To the west, there is a service from Florence to Pisa and its airport. From Pisa, the main line to the north and south along the coast serves Viareggio, Livorno and many smaller places. There are also services to Lucca. These main lines are connected to a network of minor lines weaving their way around the generally hilly area. Siena is the most prominent city served only by minor lines, best reached from the junction at Empoli by the line following the valley of the River Elsa. Other railway lines of relevance to this book include that from Lucca to Bagni di Lucca and the Garfagnana Valley, which has an organised linkage between the trains and walking in the adjacent mountains. (Leaflet 'Treno nei Parchi' from tourist information.) Services on these minor lines are generally infrequent. The Monte Amiata area has no rail service, although there is a station of that name on a minor line some distance to the north-west of the mountain.

Bus

Several different companies provide services throughout Tuscany:

Tra-in – covers a large area around Siena in the centre of the province, including San Gimignano and Volterra. Tel. 0577 204246. 'Prontorario' (instant timetable) – 0577 204270.

Sita – serves Chianti area. Tel. 055 214721

Clap – serves, Lucca, Garfagnana and the north. Tel. 0583 587897.

Rama – southern Tuscany, including Mont Amiata region. Tel. 0564 616040.

Before boarding a bus, a ticket must already have been purchased, either at a bus station or at a bar or newsagent's shop displaying the sign of the appropriate bus company. It is usually convenient to purchase a return ticket (if required) at the same time as the outward ticket. Tickets are 'validated' by stamping in the machine close to the bus entrance on boarding. Bus stops ('fermata') display the name of the company and a timetable. On the timetables look carefully for terms such as 'festivo' – Sundays and holidays, 'giornaliero' – daily, 'scolastico' – during school terms, 'Lunedi a Vendredi' – Monday to Friday, 'Sabato' – Saturday, 'Invernale' – winter, 'Cambio a ...' – change at....

Car

The majority of visitors will undoubtedly use a car, owned or hired, as the most speedy and convenient mode of travelling around the Tuscan countryside. Minor roads are generally quiet but the centres of the medieval towns and cities are often barred to all but residents' and delivery vehicles and are best avoided in any case. Cross-country journeys are comparatively slow as the roads are often narrow, winding, and up and down. Allow plenty of time for any journey and refuse to be hustled along by the local high-speed drivers. It is anathema to an Italian to follow behind another vehicle, hence a great deal of dodgy overtaking and cutting of (sometimes blind) corners. At the opposite end of the spectrum the ubiquitous workhorse, the three-wheel APE, can at times be obstructive.

Road signs and practices tend to be standard European. Signposting is generally good.

It is not uncommon for minor roads, particularly those in hilly country, to be left without a tarmac surface – 'white roads'. These are perfectly drivable but are slow, bumpy and, in dry weather, the

Touring Club sign in Radda (Walk 14)

passage of a vehicle throws up clouds of white dust. Most maps do not differentiate these roads from those with a hard surface.

Accommodation

In Tuscany, particularly in the country areas, hotels are usually of modest size and privately owned, with relatively few of the somewhat impersonal premises owned by the great international hotel chains. Inevitably, standards do vary a good deal, although there is an official 'star' rating system. It is always advisable to ask to see the room offered before acceptance. Particularly for longer stays, some form of self-catering accommodation is usually preferred. Many cottages and converted rural buildings, some of them in British ownership, are available through agencies based in Britain. Some magazines carry a range of advertisements. In recent years, there has been great development of 'Agriturismo', agricultural tourism, which can mean anything from a room in a working farm to a comprehensively equipped self-catering apartment, possibly in a holiday complex. The more sophisticated agriturismos have swimming pools and other leisure facilities.

There are youth hostels 'Ostelli della Gioventu' in the principal towns and cities. Most are open all year, but a few open only from Easter to mid October.

More than 200 camping/caravan sites cover Tuscany, with a high preponderance along the coast.

Information on all forms of accommodation is readily obtainable from tourist information offices.

Shopping

For self-caterers, food shopping is (or should be) one of the delights of an overseas holiday. Even those staying in hotels can still enjoy the purchase of the daily picnic ingredients. For most of us a supermarket, although impersonal, does provide easier selection and a greater range of goods without having to struggle with names, weights etc. in an unfamiliar language. However, Tuscany does not really have a 'supermarket culture'. Cities such as Florence and Siena do have modest supermarkets on the fringes, but for lesser towns and villages, a 'Spar'-sized shop, often owned by the Co-op, is the norm. Likewise, the great hypermarket, in the French style, is not to be found.

Shopping for clothes, gifts etc. will also be conducted in smaller, often individual, establishments, ranging from the sophisticated – Gucci, Armani and the rest – in Florence and Siena to the rustic, not forgetting the many comprehensive weekly markets. Departmental stores are rare.

In all cases, prices tend to be not very different from those in Britain, although wines and other alcoholic beverages (including Scotch whisky and English gin) are always cheaper. It has to be said that the use of the euro in place of the former lira is a big improvement in calculating relative costs of purchases.

Do remember that, with few exceptions, shops close at midday for a siesta break of about three hours.

Tourist Information

In Tuscany the various public authorities take their tourism responsibilities seriously. There are offices (ATP) in all towns of any size; even smaller places often have an office, perhaps a room in the town hall, open on a part time basis. The offices are almost always signposted within the town. In addition to having the usual array of leaflets describing local visitor attractions, staff are often able to recommend local walks. Even in the smallest office, at least some English will be spoken.

Addresses

Below are the addresses and telephone numbers of the principal relevant offices:

Regional Tourist Board – Regione Toscana, Giunta Regionale, Via di Novoli 26, 1 – 50127, Florence. Tel. (055) 438 21 11.

Via Umberto I 42, 1-55021, Bagni di Lucca. Tel. (0583) 87946

Piazza delle Erbe 1, 1-55032, Castelnuovo di Garfagnana. Tel. (0583) 65 169

Via Campana 43, 1-53034, Colle di Val d'Elsa. Tel. (0577) 91 21 11.

Costa del Municipio 8, 1-53024, Montalcino. Tel. (0577) 84 93 31.

Via Mentana 97, 1-53021, Abbadia San Salvatore (for Monte Amiata). Tel. (0577) 77 86 08.

Piazza del Duomo 1, 1-53037, San Gimignano. Tel. (0577) 94 00 08.

Piazza del Campo 56, 1-53100, Siena. Tel. (0577) 28 05 51.

Via Turazza 2, 1-56048, Volterra. Tel. (0588) 8 61 50.

Some smaller towns, e.g. Radda in Chianti, have arrangements for tourist information.

Climate

Tuscany is one of those rare favoured places where walking in the countryside is not only possible but is positively enjoyable at all times of year. Whilst the climate provides more predictable weather than is the case in the United Kingdom, there is usually sufficient variability to avoid the kind of certainty which, to British walkers, might eventually become a little monotonous despite our pleas to the contrary! Inevitably, there are a few exceptions. In winter and early spring the high ground of the Appennines, the Apuan Alps and Monte Amiata can be walked only by those experienced in, and equipped for, conditions of snow and ice, present from December to April. Otherwise, the whole of Tuscany's huge and diverse landscape is there to enjoy.

Summers are hot by our standards but do not reach tropical temperatures. Nevertheless, careful choice of routes, looking for plenty of shady woodland and, possibly, an early start to the day are recommended. As in so many parts of the world, spring and autumn provide the optimum conditions. In spring the kaleidoscopic patterns of fresh greens, embellished with early emergence of the crocuses, primroses and hundreds of other wild flowers provide truly idyllic scenery, with modest temperatures. In autumn, the greens are changing to more russet tones, but with the added interest of the wine harvest, ripening olives and still blossoming wild flowers. Temperatures remain balmy well into what we would regard as early winter.

Temperature

Typical average figures for Florence are: winter (January), 4.7°C

(40.5°F); summer (July), 24.6°C (76.3°F). Higher-lying areas are colder in both winter and summer.

Rainfall

Spring and early winter have the highest average rainfalls; January, February and July are the driest months. In such a large and diverse area the actual figures vary a great deal. In the Appennines and the Apuan Alps, 2000 – 3000mm (80 – 120") rivals the notorious rainfall of the English Lake District, whilst on part of the coast 500mm (20") drier than East Anglia, is more the norm. Central parts such as Florence and Siena receive about 840 to 860mm (33 to 34"), a little more than London or the south of England generally.

As with the British Isles, prevailing winds are mainly from the west and south, including the moisture carrying *scirocco*. In winter and early spring the *tramontana* brings a flow of cold air from the north.

Walking

In addition to the considerable number of waymarked (and sometimes numbered) walking routes, often along ancient mule tracks, farm roadways and 'white' unsurfaced roads proliferate over most of Tuscany. Very few of the farm tracks are in any way barred to walkers; indeed the general attitude of the country people seems to be quite relaxed. In total, there is great scope for country walking on walker-friendly surfaces. The white roads and even the minor hard surfaced roads carry comparatively little traffic. Route finding can occasionally pose problems, even on waymarked routes, as the placement of the marks does occasionally seem a little ambiguous. As always, route finding in woodland is less easy than elsewhere. The profusion of hunters' paths complicates what might already be a confusing situation.

Ancient routes have evolved over the centuries for long distance trade and/or pilgrimage. Passing through Tuscany are the Via Francigena, the Via Claudia and the Via Cassia. The former is perhaps the best known, linking Northern Italy and France (hence the name) with Rome, via Lucca and Siena, an authentic pilgrims' trail. The route was not geographically precise as it would be today; between different towns frequent variations were dictated by, for example, the state of rivers and fords, availability of overnight accommodation, particularly hospices, and possible local hostility. An early pilgrim was Sigeric, Archbishop of Canterbury who, in 990, travelled from Canterbury to Rome in 80 days. Sigeric crossed the Alps by the Great St Bernard Pass, following the Via

Francigena through Tuscany to Rome. Fortunately, he left notes of his journey for posterity. The route is now promoted by the tourism authorities; a booklet 'La Via Francigena in Toscana' is available in Italian, with English translation, setting out suggestions for following parts of the Via by car, bicycle or on foot.

Waymarks usually, but not always, comprise red and white stripes, similar to the French 'Grand Randonnée' marking. The 'turn left' and 'turn right' variations and the 'wrong route' cross-out are rarely seen.

None of the walks suggested includes scrambling or other difficulties; stiles and kissing gates are unlikely to be encountered. Serious mud underfoot is a rare situation in Tuscany, a dusty dryness being much more common.

There is little flat ground suitable for walkers. In the north the Garfagnana area comprises a long valley between ranges of mountains, with even the walks in the foothills rising to more than 2000ft (606m). In the very popular Chianti area, the highest point is at 2928ft (887m). The archetypical country walk among vineyards and olive groves is obviously at a lower level than this but always includes a fair amount of rise and fall, specified in the introductory information in each case. The 'crete' country and the wooded hills to the south-west of Siena are similar in their demands on the walker. In the south the extensive foothills around Monte Amiata (5704ft, 1728m) tend to produce walks with prolonged rising sections. The prevalence of hilly country is one of the reasons why the length of the walks is generally modest.

Clothing and equipment vary very little from British requirements. Suitable headwear is essential in hot sunshine and, for fair-skinned people, bare skin requires protection. Although by no means mandatory, boots are better than the alternatives. Some walkers use modern sectional walking poles, one or two at a time, as a walking aid. Whatever other reason there might be for carrying one or more poles, there is no doubt that a pole (or other stick) is a great comfort when passing farms with apparently unfriendly dogs, usually but not invariably tethered. An electronic 'dog dazer' which slips into the pocket or clips on to a belt may also be found useful. Whether or not food is to be carried, *always* carry an adequate supply of water, particularly in summer, and a basic first aid kit. In comparatively civilised countryside it might appear that a compass is hardly required but, particularly in dense woodland, the author finds one to be very useful.

Among the varieties of snake which are occasionally seen, one is poisonous. This viper is grey/brown in colour, with a diamond shaped head. Like our adder it prefers to keep itself to itself and will slip away when approaching humans are detected, biting only when provoked. Nevertheless, some authorities advise against walking in shorts and sandals.

Hunting is a deep-rooted part of the traditional countryside culture of Tuscany, with rights of way over any but fenced and usually 'divieto di caccia' (hunting prohibited) signposted land. The hunters are tough-looking men with guns and dogs, said to be ready to blast away at almost anything that moves, particularly in areas of scrub and woodland. The hunting season is from March to April. If hunting is in progress, try to make your presence apparent to the hunters.

Country code

The majority of walkers will instinctively conform to the common-sense rules of the countryside anywhere in the world and will hardly need a reminder that these apply in Tuscany. However – do leave gates as you find them; do not light fires other than at a proper fireplace; walk quietly through farms and do not alarm animals; do not leave litter; do not pick or damage wild flowers; keep to established paths wherever possible and do not walk over cultivated land; be polite and friendly to farming personnel.

Safety

Do not walk alone in remote places.

Do ensure that your equipment is adequate for the requirements of any particular walk.

Do have adequate drink (some areas are quite waterless), and emergency food (chocolate etc.)

Do check weather forecasts before going to the mountains.

Do inform someone of your intended route.

Do not stray from established tracks if there is mist.

Do carry at least a minimal first aid provision.

Do not overestimate your ability with regard to length, rise and fall and likely timing of a route.

Always regard safety as first priority. Carabinieri and mountain rescue – tel 112, Fire – 115, Ambulance – 118. Tel 113 in cases of the most serious emergency.

Maps

For Tuscany there is no coherent set of maps for walkers which can in any way be compared with our Ordnance Survey Outdoor Leisure and Explorer series. The variety of producers, the different ranges which they publish and the rather haphazard availability through newsagents and bookshops all contribute to a situation of buying whatever is on offer and seems best for a particular area at a particular time. Those quoted in respect of the various walks in this book are generally the best that could be obtained locally. For advance purchase, The Map Shop at 15, High Street, Upton upon Severn, Worcestershire WR8 0HJ, tel. 01684 593146, does have Italian maps in stock and does provide a speedy and helpful postal service.

Edizioni Multigraphic of Florence seems to be the largest Tuscany map producing company with, for our purposes, ranges at scales of 1:50 000 and 1:25 000. The former include Carta Turistica Stradale, primarily road maps, but with Sentieri C.A.I. (designated Italian Alpine Club footpaths) included. Despite this inclusion, these maps cannot be recommended. By the same company, the Carta Territoriale at the same scale is only a little better. Much to be preferred are series at 1:25 000 – Carta Turistica e dei Sentieri and Sentieri della Provincia di Siena, which are broadly similar to one another.

Other maps worth having are the German-produced Kompass series, but unfortunately at the less good 1:50 000 scale. Routes organised by the Province of Siena are particularly well marked. The maps in the 1:50 000 Wanderkarte series by another German company, Freytag & Berndt are moderately useful.

Always obtain maps at 1:25 000 scale if possible

Walkers' Glossary

abbazia (or badia)	abbey
autobus	bus
borro	watercourse
bosco	woodland
cana	dog
casa	house, home
castel, castello	castle
chiesa	parish church
cimitero	cemetery
citta	town, city
col, colle, passo	pass
collina	hill
destro	right
duomo	cathedral
est	east
fattoria	farm
fiume	river
fonte (or sorgente)	spring

fortezza	fortress
fosso	small valley or watercourse
grotta	cave
lago	lake
monte, montagna	mountain
mulattiera	mule track
nebbia	fog, mist
neve	snow
nord	north
ovest	west
pioggia	rain
pizzo	peak
podere	farm or estate
poggio	knoll
ponte	bridge
porta	gate, doorway
rifugio	mountain hut
rocca	fortress (usually ruined)
sentiero	footpath
sinistra	left
sole	sun
sopra	high
sotto	low
stazione	station
strada	road
strata privata	private road
sud	south
tabernacolo	shrine
tomba	tomb
torrente	stream
treno	train
valle	valley
via	road/street
villaggio	village

Don't forget the niceties:

Good day	*buon giorno*
Hello	*Salve*
Mr/Mrs	*Signore/Signora*
Please	*per favore*
Thank you	*grazie*
Goodbye	*arrivederci*
Don't mention it	*prego*
Hello/cheerio	*ciao*

Opposite: Santa Fiora, Walk 1

The South

1. Santa Fiora – Monte Amiata

A circuit around some of the immense wooded slopes of the great mountain, following a variety of forest roadways and paths. Inevitably there are long ascents and corresponding descents, some of which are quite steep.

Distance: 9km (5½ miles) or 10km (6¼ miles) with diversion. Total ascent: 1300ft (394m).

Start/car parking: A small off-road space in front of the redundant church of S. Rocco, on the northern fringe of Santa Fiora. From the town centre cross the high bridge then take the second turn on the left to head directly to S. Rocco church (which does not display its name). If approaching from Arcidosso turn sharp left just before the town centre and follow the road as it bends round to the right to reach S. Rocco in less than half a mile.

Refreshments: Café/bars in Santa Fiora.

Maps: Multigraphic, Monte Amiata. Val d'Orcia, Sentieri e Rifugi, 1:25 000. Freytag & Berndt WKI 30, Chianciano – Valdichiana – Monte Amiata, Wanderkarte, 1:50 000.

The Walk

Walk along the roadside, away from Santa Fiora, for about 50 metres before turning into a well-waymarked track on the left, rising quite steeply. Pass a property, still rising. Go straight across a more major track and along a gully-like section before passing another house. The track leads to a logging area of forest, where the previously reliable waymarks are not in evidence. Go straight across this area and along a narrow path at the far side, where a waymark will soon be found. *The mountain ahead is Poggio Trauzzolo (3938ft) around which our route circles.*

1. Continue the steady ascent along a broad track, passing stone buildings 100 metres to the left of the route. Continue upwards, heading generally north – this is the most demanding section of the circuit. Near the top, at a junction, bear round to the right, now heading north of east. Pass another junction.

2. At a cross paths in less than half a mile turn right. In 50 metres, turn left to resume the previous direction, gently downhill.

3. At the next junction, a turn to the right continues the circuit. *The attractive path going straight on at this point leads to a*

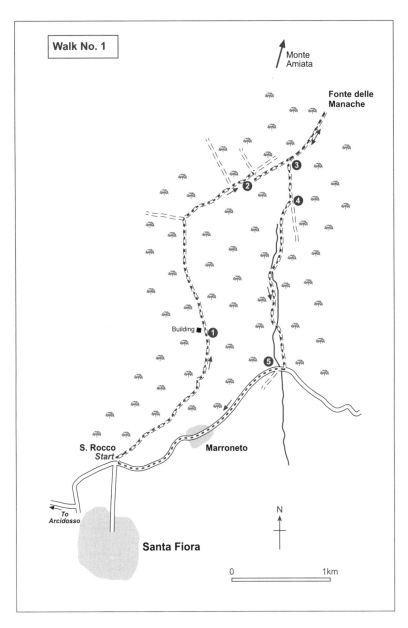

Walk No. 1

Monte
Amiata

Fonte delle
Manache

❸

❷

❹

Building ■ ❶

❺

S. Rocco
Start

Marroneto

*To
Arcidosso*

Santa Fiora

N

0   1km

*spring – the Fonte delle Monache. If visiting the spring, return
by the same route for a diversion totalling just over a kilometre.*
Otherwise, carry on downhill for about half a mile.

4. Fork right at a path heading down the side of the valley, reaching a dry stream bed by some huge boulders in 100m. Bear left

along a delightful woodland path, staying close to the valley bottom for a considerable distance, twice crossing the streambed. The path gradually becomes a wider forest track. After passing an area of commercial woodland activity, bear right to pass behind a small factory complex and join a minor public road

5. Follow the road to the right, soon forking right, uphill, along a road which, for some distance is without tarmac; this road passes through the residential suburb of Marroneto, on its way to S. Rocco. Keep left at a fork and carry on to return to the parking area.

Santa Fiora

Places of interest

Santa Fiora is arguably the most attractive of the string of small towns along the base of Monte Amiata, best seen from below, where rows of old houses perching one above the other, connected by narrow streets and alleyways, climb the side of a steep cliff of trachyte rock. In medieval times, the town was part of the great possessions of the Aldobrandeschi family. In 1439, as a result of marriage, control passed into the hands of another family and eventually to distant Florence 1633. The cliff is crowned by the Palace del Conte, now the municipal headquarters. Quite fascinating is the roadway, including a flight of steps, through this ancient building. Behind the palace is a sizable piazza from which the keep of the Aldobrandeschi castle can be seen. Close by is the bridge high over a deep valley, a good viewpoint. Across the piazza from the palace, the Via Carolina leads to the 18th-century church of Suffragio before descending sharply to the Chapel of Santa Fiora. Originally built before AD 1000, rebuilt in AD 1200 and enlarged in 1792, the chapel has a famed collection of terracottas attributed to Andrea della Robbia. After visiting the church it is worth continuing on the little roadway down the face of the cliff to the attractive 'Great Fishpond' at the bottom. Included within the wall which encircles the pond is a small garden.

Only 5 miles (8km) to the north-west of Santa Fiora, the larger town of Arcidosso is similarly rich in medieval features, including yet another structure by those indefatigable castle builders the Aldobrandeschi. The even larger town and famous abbey of San. Salvatore lie 9 miles (14km) to the north-east of Santa Fiora.

Monte Amiata is the great landmark of southern Tuscany. A long extinct volcano, it rises to a height of 5704ft, its great slopes heavily wooded but with some areas near the top cleared for ski lifts. As the slopes are nowhere precipitous, the mountain covers an enormous area of land, a huge bulk which has always dominated most aspects of life in these parts. It is possible to drive to the summit where there are hotels and other facilities. There is of course a great deal of snow and ice in winter, lingering until well into spring.

Five miles west of Santa Fiora the extensive Parco Faunistico del Monte Amiata is a low-key visitor attraction, reached along unsurfaced roadways. A variety of animals is kept on an expanse of natural countryside. Check carefully for opening hours.

Other walks

Walk 2 in this book

Varied circuits on and around Monte Amiata (local map available at tourist information offices).

2. Castel del Piano and Seggiano

A fine linear walk connecting two of the small towns/villages situated low on the western flank of Monte Amiata. The route is a little more hilly than might be expected but the interest of the diverse countryside, the olives, the vines and the agriculture, is ample recompense. The splendid views of the hill village of Montegiovi, Potentino Castle, Monte Amiata and back to Seggiano are all bonuses. Good tracks and waymarking throughout, with very little public road. Shade is scanty.

The route lends itself well to a return by public transport. The RADA bus for Seggiano departs from the bus shelter in front of the Co-op store in Castle del Piano at 13.30, 15.15 and 18.55 (the latter not on Sundays). (It is always advisable to check times!).

Distance: 9km (5½ miles). Total ascent: 1200ft (364m).

Start/car parking: High up in the hill village of Seggiano is a small parking area close to a bus shelter

Refreshments: Bar at foot of hill in Seggiano. Choice of several in Castel del Piano.

Maps: Multigraphic, Monte Amiata, Val d'Orcia, Sentieri e Rifugi, 1:25 000. Freytag & Berndt WKI 30, Chianciano. Valdichiana. Monte Amiato, 1:50 000.

The Walk

Just beyond the parking area is a walking route board and a waymark indicating the start of this walk, Go steeply downhill, soon bearing right. Turn right along a waymarked grass path before reaching the bottom of the hill. The path curves around the hillside below Seggiano before joining a surfaced roadway beside an industrial building. Con-

Castel del Piano

tinue downhill, passing a small furniture works on the way to a road junction.

22

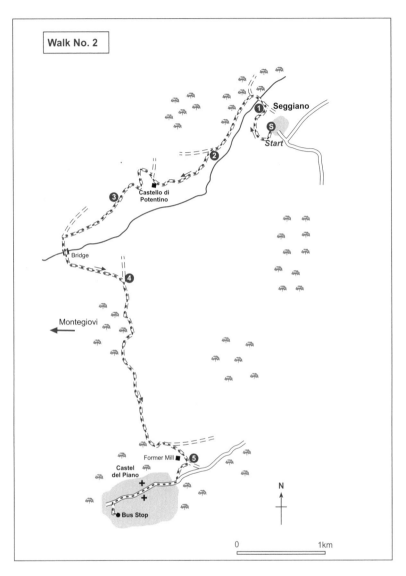

Walk No. 2

1. Join the road, cross a bridge over the Concia stream and turn left along a minor road, signposted 'Oratorio del Columbaio'. *There are glimpses of Seggiano, high on the left.* The road ascends the valley side, above the gurgling stream – an attractive and not too common accompaniment to a Tuscan walk.

2. As the road sweeps up to the right, take an unsurfaced roadway on the left, passing a large 'Agriturismo'. Descend the valley side. To the left is a tiny stone building – the former oratory as

23

signposted, with what appears to be the base of a cross in front? Pass below a grove of very old olive trees and approach Potentino Castle. Bear right to pass the castle and through vineyards. Keep left at a fork 100 metres after the castle. At the next fork go right to rise again. Go straight on at subsequent forks, staying with the main track.

3. Reach the crest of a ridge, going straight ahead at a junction. There are now long views to the west as we head for Montegiovi, with quite a long descent to the valley bottom. Cross the stream on a bridge to rise up the far side of the valley. Bear right at a fork to follow ' Sodi' and 'Casale'. Pass an old house and continue. Pass a stone hut and fork left by a new house (the waymark is 50 metres ahead). Reach tarmac and ascend past a house up to a road junction.

4. Turn right here, now downhill, heading for Castel del Piano, formidably high in front. Stay on the tarmac road to pass a derelict house; the road soon rises steeply. Pass a former mill, Moline delle Conce, below on the right.

5. At a ruined building in a few metres, turn tightly to the right along an unsurfaced track, cross a stream on a bridge and turn left, steeply uphill, to reach the edge of Castel del Piano. Continue along Via Pianetta, passing a former wash trough on the left. Cross a small piazza and carry on along Corso Nasini, the main street of the older part of the town. *To visit the really old quarter, turn up to the right past the prominent clock tower.* Pass two churches and continue along the side of the large Piazza Garibaldi to reach another huge square, with central gardens. The Co-op store with bus shelter outside, is a few metres to the left.

Places of interest

The ancient town of Castel del Piano is quite small, close packed by the Tower of the Clock and the small square of the Ortaggi with its beautiful 16th-century loggia. The newer, much more extensive, part of the town was laid out early in the 20th century, with two great piazzas, interesting monuments and wide, tree-lined, avenues.

Castel was the home town of the Nasini family, no less than seven of whom were actively painting in the area from the 17th to the mid-18th centuries. The church of Proposituria di Saints Nicholas and Lucia, which was completed in 1870 in a Baroque style, is very much a museum of the family's art.

Sitting on the top and up the side of a sharp hill, old Seggiano has little spare space for anything other than houses, a municipal palace and the churches of St Bartholomew and Corpus Domini. The former has works of art dating from the mid-14th century, whilst the latter has paintings of the Sienese school, spanning the period from the 14th to the 18th centuries. At the foot of the hill a few shops and a café/bar huddle in the newer part of the village.

Other walks

Walks 1 and 3 in this book

Many walks on Monte Amiata (map from tourist information offices).

3. Vivo d'Orcia

Another opportunity to tramp around the immense wooded slopes, this time on the north side, of Monte Amiata, the great extinct volcano which dominates south-east Tuscany. Beech, chestnut and pine predominate. Inevitably the route is largely up and down, on broad forest tracks and unsurfaced roadways, but is without very steep gradients.

Distance: 10km (6¼ miles). Total ascent: 1300ft (394m).

Start/car parking: There are several off-street car parks in the little town of Vivo d'Orcia. Reach Vivo along minor roads north-east of Castel del Piano or north-west from Abbadia San Salvatore.

Refreshments: Café/bar in Vivo d'Orcia.

Maps: Multigraphic, Val d'Orcia, Sentieri della Provincia di Siena, 1:25 000. Freytag & Berndt WKI 30, Chianciano. Valdichiana. Monte Amiata, 1:50 000.

Walk

From any car park in Vivo, walk to the crossroads in the middle of the village and start along the road signposted to Abbadia San Salvatore. At the first bend, in 60m, fork right, steeply uphill towards a modern church. Opposite the church fork right, by a walkers' route board. Pass the front of a school, where the road-way loses its surface. Descend and, in 200 metres, bear right, down the valley side on a rough path. Cross the top of a concrete dam. *There is pretty rock scenery and a pool in this charming little valley.* Go up steps and turn right to pass an area with picnic tables. *To see a waterfall there is a diversion to the left.*

1. Meet a wide gravel track, turning left, uphill (red and white waymark). Pass overhanging cliffs before joining a public road. Turn left along the road, then left again in 50 metres to follow an unsurfaced roadway. There are signposts including 'Sorgente di Vivo' and 'Ermicciolo'. The ascent cuts a wide swathe through the pine forest.

2. At a waymarked junction turn right to pass between old gate-posts, then pass a jumble of great rocks. At a junction, stay with the main track, round to the right. At another junction, with a 'route 11' waymark, go straight on, slightly downhill, passing more great boulders. Pass a waterworks structure built into the

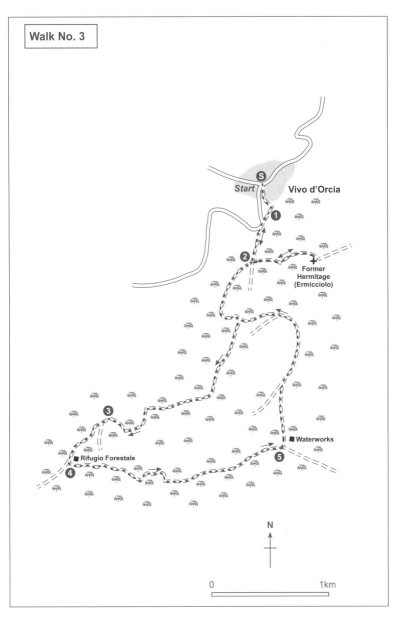

Walk No. 3

Start

Vivo d'Orcia

Former
Hermitage
(Ermicciolo)

Rifugio Forestale

Waterworks

N

0   1km

rocks then, in 250 metres, as the track bends to the right, take a well-waymarked minor path on the left, rising between the trees.

3. Close to another waterworks building leave the path as it ascends by a dry stream bed, making a sharp right turn to pass

Rifugio Forestale "Caprovetra"

along the side of the building (waymarks). In 100 metres, join another path, turning left. Cross a dribbly little stream and then a more open area, rich in broom, with long views to Castiglione. The stone-built Rifugio Caprovetra is soon reached.

4. Go round the Rifugio, raking back to the left to follow 'route 10' along a rising path which stays below beech woods and a minor road for some distance. Join the road momentarily then go left immediately to pass a post and chain barrier before crossing an open area to find waymarks on the far side. Bear left up a sunken track. At a junction turn left then, in 10 metres, bear right. Ignore tracks to right and left and continue to head east, passing some striking rocks. About a mile from the Rifugio reach a junction close to substantial waterworks buildings.

5. Turn left towards the buildings (waymarks) and continue along a rough, unsurfaced, roadway. The excellent track descends gently; at a bend there are waymarks on trees. Pass a little hut. The roadway winds considerably before passing spectacular rocks. Bear right at a junction here. Rejoin the outward route at a waymarked junction, turning right to return towards Vivo by the same route. (Don't forget to fork right 50 metres after joining the public road)

At the junction by the old gate posts (point 2), a diversion along the broad rising track to the right leads to the Ermicciolo (hermitage) in about 800 metres, passing picnic areas on the way. Return by the same route.

Places of interest

One of the highest towns/villages on the extended Monte Amiata, Vivo d'Orcia has the Hermitage del Vivo, a late Renaissance building facing the valley below, constructed as a palace in the 16th century on the site of the former monastic structure. In the not very exciting town centre, the church of S. Marcello has interesting paintings.

L'Ermicciolo was originally a 13th-century Romanesque chapel, considerably rebuilt in the 19th century, with a decorative colonnade on the façade. It is sited in the heart of a magnificent chestnut forest. The two adjacent stone buildings are chestnut drying sheds, used at chestnut harvest time each year.

Campiglia d'Orcia is another of the smaller, tranquil, towns to the north of the mountain. The principal point of interest is the ruin of the fortress constructed in 973, demolished by the Sienese in 1234. Only part of a limestone tower remains. The medieval church of S. Biagio, rebuilt many times, has a fine work by Sebastian Folli (1560 – 1621).

Other walks

Walks 2, 4 and 5 in this book.

Network of marked trails around Monte Amiata (map from tourist information offices).

'Walking the Val d'Orcia' – booklet (in English) from tourist information offices.

4. Castiglione d'Orcia

A circular walk which reverses the march of the Duke of York's men. This is inevitable, as the route is based on the lovely little hill town of Castiglione, with the adjacent valley of the River Orcia as the destination. Good tracks and unsurfaced roadways predominate. The uphill return is prolonged and generally steep. The views, mainly across the Orcia valley, are splendid.

Distance: 6.5km (4 miles). Total ascent: 1320ft (400m).

Start/car parking: Small free car park by the side of the main road, which skirts round the old centre of Castiglione, at the south end. Castiglione is reached by a short diversion from the main road, SS2, from Siena towards Rome, about 3 miles (5km) south of San Quirico.

Refreshments: Café/bar beside the car park in Castiglione.

Map: Multigraphic, Val d'Orcia, Sentieri della Provincia di Siena, 1:25 000.

The Walk

Cross the main road and bear right, up the street opposite, following signs for 'farmacia', 'posta' etc. The street is Borgio Vittorio Emmanuelle. Keep to this long street through Castiglione. *Above, to the left is the ruin of a castle.* Rejoin the main road, turning left for a short distance.

1. Opposite a filling station and the Carabinieri, turn left into the Via della Rocca. Take a left turn into the Via del Olivetto at a staggered crossroads.

2. A little way past a Fiat service station and a small bakery, descend through a small car park before bending sharp right in 50 metres, to

Church at Castiglione d'Orcia

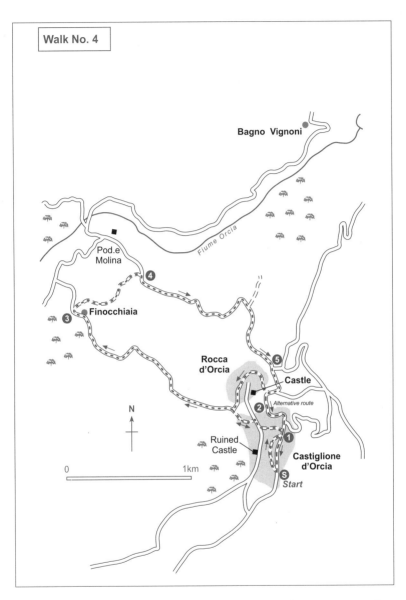

Walk No. 4

Bagno Vignoni

Fiume Orcia

Pod.e Molina

④

③ ●Finocchiaia

Rocca d'Orcia

⑤

Castle

Alternative route

②

N

↑

Ruined Castle

①

Castiglione d'Orcia

0   1km

Ⓢ *Start*

descend steeply below the 13th-century castle on its mound to the right. At a junction at the bottom, turn left to pass a 'no through road' sign and continue the descent. The road loses its surface before rising a little. Keep right at a major fork, descending. Pass above a farm and through light woodland. *The Orcia valley views are extensive, including the castle at Ripa d'Orcia on the far side of the river.*

Agriculture

The understandable concentration on wine and olives tends to over-look the considerable importance of arable farming in Tuscany, where medium to large farms produce grain (largely for pasta!), fruit, vegetables and sunflowers. Livestock farming is comparatively minor. As mentioned under 'wine', the present situation emerged from the collapse of the centuries old 'mezzadria' system whereby the absentee landowner bore 50% of the costs of seed and other essentials in return for 50% of the crops which the peasant farmer produced from the land.

A notable landscape feature is the system of terraces which form parallel lines across so many Tuscan hillsides, mostly built centuries ago to provide comparatively level ground and better depth of soil on a series of 'steps', enabling the peasant farmers to grow a variety of crops, including vines, on otherwise almost useless ground. Nowadays, apart from olive trees, the terraces lie neglected as other crops are economic only when cultivated with mechanical aid, usually not possible on the terraces. In many cases the stone-built retaining walls are still in fair condition.

3. Descend to a farm and, in less than 100 metres, look out carefully for a broad track on the right, below a barn. Turn right here to continue the descent, above a house on the left, with a glimpse of the Orcia River.

4. At a 'T' junction turn right to commence the long ascent to Castiglione on an unsurfaced road. The route now has red and white waymarks at frequent intervals. *Rocca, fort and village, is an awesome spectacle ahead.* Towards the top of the hill is a farmstead, Podere Colombaiolo, with a prominent well on the right. Bear left for a short distance to join a road with 'Siena' and 'Castiglione' signs. Turn right along the road. At a junction turn right again following a 'Rocca d'Orcia' signpost.

5. At another junction in 100 metres, *the road to the left provides the shortest and easiest return to Castiglione and the car park.* However, a turn to the right to walk through the marvellous little village of Rocca, perched on the cliffside, is highly recommended. In the village, carry on through a piazza with a great well. At the far end of Rocca descend to the junction at point 2. of the outward route and turn left to retrace your steps to the car park, either through the old centre of Castiglione or by a short cut along the main road.

Places of interest

The compact medieval town of Castiglione stands on the crest of the south bank of the well-known Val d'Orcia. The cobbled piazza and nice old buildings are crowned by the ruins of a fortress, one of the strongholds of the celebrated Aldobrandeschi family, who held sway over this part of Tuscany. The parish church has Madonnas by three of the great Sienese artists.

Rocca is a quiet medieval village which, seen from below, appears to be plastered to the side of the great rock on which stands the imposing fortress, open to the public.

Other walks

Walk 5, on the far side of the Orcia valley is very close indeed. So much so that it can be coupled with this walk to make a long, hard, circuit, crossing the river close to the abandoned bridges.

The Province of Siena leaflet 'Walking the Val d'Orcia' is a guide to the trails of this part of the Province, offering a total of nine routes, with English text. It should be available at tourist information offices.

5. Bagno Vignoni

One of the most popular walks in Tuscany, this fine circuit is based on the spa village of Bagno Vignoni. The route starts by following the valley of the Orcia River before climbing the valley side and returning over high ground with extensive views. Underfoot, unsurfaced roadways and woodland cart tracks predominate. The ascent of the valley side totals about 740ft (224m) but the gradient is moderate. The higher part of the walk has very little shade.

Distance: 10km (6¼ miles); add 1.3km (1 mile) for the diversion to Ripa. Total ascent: 900ft (273m).

Start/car parking: Car parks (some free) at Bagno Vignoni. For Bagno Vignoni, turn to the west off the main SS2, Sienna towards Rome, road about 3 miles (5km) south of San Quirico.

Refreshments: Cafés/bars in Bagno Vignoni.

Map: Multigraphic, Val d'Orcia Sentieri della Provincia di Siena, 1:25 000.

The Walk

From the car parking area at Bagno Vignoni walk to the top of the cliff down which the warm water from the thermal springs flows in a channel. Use a steep path to the left of the water flow to descend the cliff side (*or walk back down the Bagno Vignoni access road then turn sharp right along a lane if you don't like the steep slope*). In either case you reach the foot of the remarkable lime-encrusted rocks, an almost lunar landscape. *There is a pool of tepid water at the bottom in which bathing is possible.*

1. Continue along the broad track, following the line of the River Orcia, with a view of the castle at Rocca on the far side. *The vegetation is a Mediterranean scrub mixture – 'maquis'.* Pass the ruins of a tiny mill and reach the site of a former travertine quarry, its buildings sadly derelict and with an unlovely spoil heap. Stay with the main track through this area. The castle at Ripa d'Orcia comes into view ahead as the route narrows to become a path through light woodland. Go along the bottom edge of a large field, approaching the now audible river.

2. At a junction marked by a map on a board, the route continues to the right, *but a highly recommended diversion to the left goes to the riverside in a few metres. At this point is the formerly important connection to the Castiglione route. The road bridge*

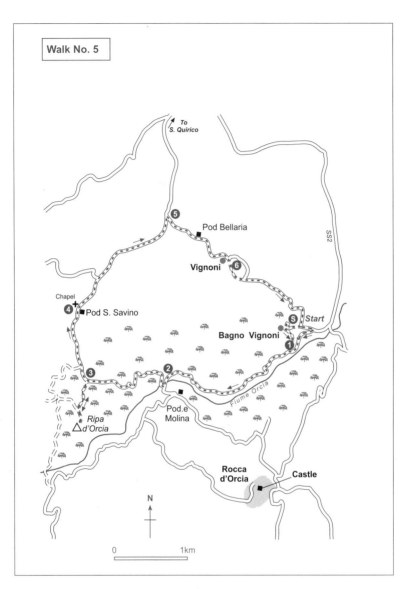

Walk No. 5

To S. Quirico

Pod Bellaria

Vignoni

Chapel

Pod S. Savino

Bagno Vignoni

Start

Flume Orcia

Pod.e Molina

Ripa d'Orcia

Rocca d'Orcia

Castle

N

0   1km

SS2

was washed away in floods many years ago and the pedestrian suspension bridge is missing much of its decking. A crossing of the shallow water using the concrete top of a weir/big stones/paddling is perfectly reasonable unless the river is in spate. Return to the junction. Carry on across a tiny stream and go uphill, commencing the long ascent (red and white waymark) through light woodland. At a 'T' junction turn right to continue the ascent (waymarked). At another apparent 'T'

Bagno Vignoni: the hot pool

junction go right (waymark on rock) passing an olive grove and with longer views over farmland.

3. Join an unsurfaced road by a water tap, turning right. *A left turn here reaches the castle at Ripa d'Orcia in about 800 metres. The castle now functions as a hotel/restaurant; there are superb views of the Orcia valley from a footpath below the castle walls.* Back on course, rise more gently past Agriturismo farmhouses, with direct sales of wine and olives. At the top of the rise there is a tiny wayside chapel on the left and another Agriturismo on the right.

4. Bear right here; the views now extend over a whole new area of countryside, including Montalcino and a good deal of the Siena 'crete'. Continue along the unsurfaced road, rising gently along a broad ridge, with the occasional waymark to confirm the route. Keep right at a road junction, gently uphill, passing two farms, one apparently deserted. At 1750ft.you are now at the crest of the walk. *San Quirico is in view, left/ahead, whilst over the Orcia valley Monte Amiata provides a distant but impressive backdrop.* Head towards San Quirico, descending a little.

5. Turn sharp right along a similar roadway, rising a little to pass a

small pond and a farm before starting the long downhill return, heading first to the compact medieval hamlet of Vignone, sandwiched between a solidly built tower at the near end and the church at the far end. At a fork just before the hamlet, *turn right to bypass or* go ahead to walk along the tiny street.

6. Go through the arch at the far end of the street and turn right to follow a little path, rejoining the roadway by the cemetery. Turn left to continue, passing abundant wild broom on this steep descent, then a very old but beautifully restored farm, still steeply downhill. Join the Bagno Vignoni access road, turning right to return to the car parking area.

Places of interest

The ancient village of Bagno Vignoni has long been famed for the therapeutic value of the mineral-rich warm spring water. A Latin inscription in the travertine at the base of the left wing of the spa confirms the claimed Roman origin. The water comes from a depth of 1000m at a temperature of 52°C, feeding a pool 49m by 29m. It has long been recommended for maladies of the skeletal system, the mucosa and the skin. Both St Catherine of Siena and Lorenzo

Flowers and trees in Tuscany

The importance of the wealth of wild flowers which contribute much to this landscape, from the very early spring when crocuses, primroses and a score of others line the tracks, through to a very late autumn, is now well recognised by the authorities. Together with the rich wildlife it has provided motivation for the creation of a considerable range of nature reserves, no less than 103 scattered throughout the region. Many are on or close to the coast, whilst others are spread throughout inland Tuscany, including a fair number in the mountains. Two have the status of National Parks; four are Regional/Provincial Parks. The remainder are a mixture of nature reserves of state/regional importance and protected areas of local interest.

As would be expected with such geographical diversity, the variety of both flora and fauna is vast. There are huge areas of beech, oak, chestnut and pine woodland, particularly around Monte Amiata, to the south west of Siena and covering the Monti di Chianti. Alders, willow and ash are particularly evident by the sides of rivers and streams. Most characteristic are the cypresses and umbrella pines, planted from time immemorial to mark agricultural and other boundaries. The widespread maquis type vegetation is rich in wild broom, its acid yellow flowers brightening the otherwise dull scrub. Orchids are prominent among the claimed 8000 different types of flower in Tuscany.

the Magnificent (of the Medici family) were clients. The great pool is no longer used for bathing but there is an outdoor pool at the Hotel Posta Marcucci nearby, open to non-residents. Alternatively you can find the little pool at the foot of the cliff for free bathing.

San Quirico d'Orcia is three miles (5km) north of Bagno, a walled medieval town with some modern suburbs, an important centre on the ancient Via Francigena. Worth seeing are the Collegiata, rebuilt in the 12th century, the Chigi Palace of 1600 and a great park which includes a 16th-century ornamental garden.

A few miles to the east, even more renowned, is the charming town of Pienza, constructed by a member of the celebrated Piccolomini family who became Pope Pius II in 1458. The village of his birth, Corisgnano, was transformed into a model new town by the architect Bernado Rossellino in the remarkably short space of time between 1459 and 1462. Unsurprisingly, the central square is named Piazza Pio II. It is flanked by the cathedral of Santa Maria Assunta, the Palazzo Vescovile (Bishop's Palace), the Palazzo Piccolomini and the Palazzo Comunale.

Beyond Pienza is Montepulciano, a name known worldwide from millions of labels on wine bottles. Quite apart from the reputation of its wines, Montepulciano is a fine, larger, walled hill town of ancient (likely Etruscan) origins. A grand piazza, several renaissance palaces, a cathedral and a civic museum all contribute to its overall attraction.

Castiglione d'Orcia – see walk 4

Other walks

Walk 4 in this book

Provincia di Siena booklet 'Walking the Val d'Orcia' (in English) from tourist information centres. Nine routes in this part of the Province.

Cloister at Torri (Walk 11)

South/Central

6. Sant'Antimo Abbey

*An approach on foot to one of Tuscany's great abbeys,
beautifully set in a depression against a backdrop of a wooded
hillside. A very straightforward track, part of the Siena Province
route no. 2, descends directly to the abbey from the adjacent
hills, the south end of the 'Crete' country. There are steep
sections of the track which could be a little slippery in wet
weather.*

Distance: 6km (3¾ miles). Total ascent: 740ft (224m).

Start/car parking: The walk starts at the remote hamlet of Villa
Tolli, reached via an unsurfaced road which, from Montalcino
direction, is a left turn from the road to Grosseto. About 3
miles (5km) south of Montalcino there is a big left-hand bend.
The left turn is a short distance after a road joins from the right
and is signposted to many places, including Villa a Tolli.
Parking at the hamlet is not too easy; driving a little further
towards S. Antimo there are better roadside areas.

Refreshments: Picnic only.

Map: Multigraphic, Sentieri della Provincia di Siena, Val d'
Orcia, 1:25 000.

The Walk

From Villa a Tolli, or a little further down the access road, carry on
towards Sant'Antimo. At a junction with the entrance drive to
Fattoria Magia, dip to the left to descend steadily and sometimes
steeply along a broad sandy track. Route finding is very simple; as
part of a numbered Siena Province walk, the route is well
waymarked. Keep to the main track at any junction and enjoy the
superb views – great swathes of countryside across to the Crete
hills, the Appenines and Monte Amiata, an extinct volcano peak-
ing at 5704ft (1738m). The vegetation is largely light woodland,
sparse in many sections, with dense broom. It is home to lizards
and the occasional snake. Keep going downhill, fork left at a junction near the bottom and reach the Abbey. Unless there is a
non-walking driver or two vehicles, return to Villa by the same
route. *A possible alternative return route is shown on the sketch
map.*

Places of interest

It is believed that the first abbey on the site of Sant 'Antimo dated
from AD 813 and was founded by Charlemagne. It soon became a

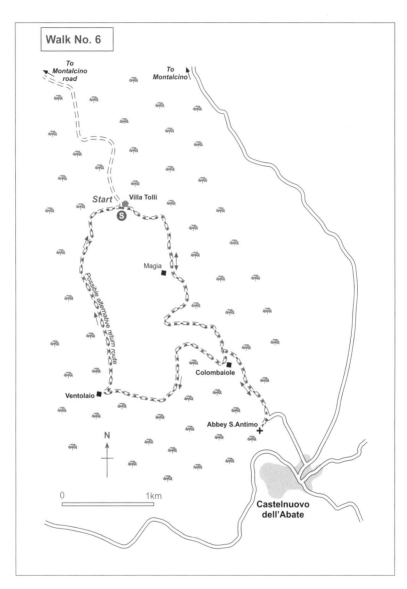

Walk No. 6

To Montalcino road

To Montalcino

Start
Villa Tolli
(S)

Possible alternative return route

Magia

Colombaiole

Ventolaio

Abbey S.Antimo

N

0   1km

Castelnuovo dell'Abate

powerful Benedictine institution with widespread land ownership and a destination for pilgrims using the Via Francigena. Generous donations in 1117 resulted in the construction of a fine large abbey, of which only the church now remains. Unfortunately, a general deterioration resulted in suppression by Pope Pious II in 1462. However, the church building, constructed in travertine stone in uncluttered Romanesque style, has been maintained in a sound condition and some services are still held by a small group

Sant'Antimo abbey

of monks. Noteworthy are the richly decorated doorway and the carved capitals, some with plant and animal motifs. Daniel in the lions' den (second column on the right) is particularly striking.

Villa Tolli is an unpretentious hamlet with a wooden cross and a small church at the rear.

Other walks

Province of Siena route no. 2 connects with walks 4 and 5 in this book.

Siena (see walks 10 and 12)

Castel del Piano (Walk 2)

Hotel Castellina, in Chianti

Trees and landscape near Volpaia (Walk 16)

Brolio Castle (Walk 15)

San Gimignano (Walk 21)

Bagno Vignoni (Walk 5)

Cloister, Torri (Walk 11)

San Donato (Walk 19)

San Galgano (Walk 7)

Pisa: the Baptistry

Pisa: the leaning tower

Olive grove, Murlo (Walk 8)

Old terraces, Chianti

Monteriggioni: shopping (Walk 13)

Monteriggioni, café scene (Walk 13)

7. San Galgano

A rare opportunity to play the role of a pilgrim without making the effort to walk all the way to Santiago del Compostella or even to Canterbury! The more modest destination of San Galgano is reached via a very easy, almost level, 2½-mile (4km) track. Apart from a little mud in wet weather the route is first rate underfoot and is also easy to follow. Unless arrangements are made with two cars or a non-walking driver, the same route is used for the return (as did most pilgrims!). There is a (very infrequent) bus service

Distance: 8km (5 miles) return. Total ascent: 150ft (45m).

Start/car parking: Small car park in Palazetto village. Palazetto is on the SS441, Siena to Massa Marittima road, 2 miles (3km) south-west of the road turning for San Galgano abbey. The car park is signposted from the main road through the village, by the side of the bar/café Palazetto.

Refreshments: Bar/café (and grocery) at Palazetto. Bar/café at San Galgano

Map: Multigraphic, Chianti e Colline Senesi, 1:50 000.

The Walk

From the car park walk back to the main road. Go straight across, then along a little road opposite. Pass a '5' waymark in a few metres. Continue to the end of this road then go right, round the corner of a house, and through a little gate with 'S. Galgano' painted on. This is the end of the route finding for this walk! Follow a broad grass track heading for a derelict farmstead. There are (unnecessary) waymarks on every electricity post. Keep to the left of the buildings and take a track with a 'strada privata' notice.

1. The track now heads straight across an arable field. *There are well-shaped hills of about 1700ft (515m) visible to the right.* At the far end of the field go left then right through a gap in a hedge and continue along the right hand edge of another arable field. Enter light woodland, largely of rather scrubby oaks, the prevailing vegetation for most of the way. Ignore all forks and keep to the main track all the way to the abbey. *In early spring crocuses are plentiful and the occasional porcupine quill is evidence of the presence of these elusive creatures.* The way is predominantly gently downhill. Pass a little pond on the left. Derelict farm buildings soon come into view, with the abbey behind.

San Galgano

2. Go round to the left in front of the farm buildings (waymark on short concrete stump) and rise quite steeply towards the abbey.

3. An extension of the walk leading up the hill behind the abbey for a short distance to the charming circular church claimed to be on the actual site of San Galgano's hermitage is highly recommended.

    Return to Palazetto by the same route unless other arrangements have been made

    Footnote – The track is, in reality, much more likely to be a 'Via Maremma', an ancient drovers' route rather than a true pilgrims' way. Livestock was moved in large numbers from the hilly pastures down to the warmer, more lush, expanses of the Maremma each winter, using a network of such tracks.

Places of interest

San Galgano was a 12th-century hermit residence on what is now the site of the circular church. Work on the construction of the great abbey started in 1218, was finished in 1262 and consecrated in 1288. The great structure is regarded as the best example of Cistercian gothic in Italy. The unfortunate spiritual and structural decay of the 16th century led to removal of the roof in the late 18th century. Proper conservation and stabilization of the remains was carried out in 1926.

The circular church 'Capella di Montesiepi' was started in

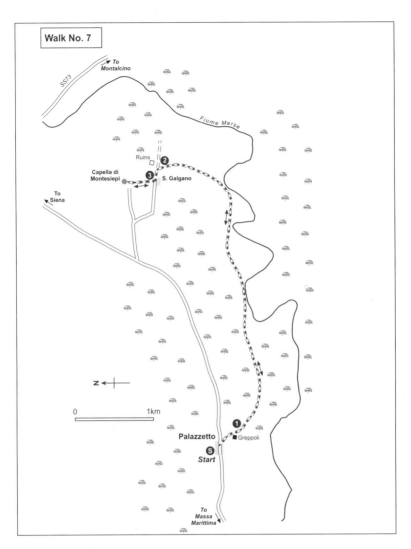

1185. There is an interesting exhibit of a sword thrust into a stone, symbolizing San Galgano's conversion from a warrior to a man of God.

Other walks

Province of Siena numbered route 7 heads north through Pentolina to link with other walks in this book in the area of Stigliano and Torri.

8. Murlo and Miniera

This circuit, based on the ancient hamlet of Murlo, has a fair amount of up and down, one descent being steep. Underfoot there are no significant problems. Part of the lengthy initial section on (quiet) public road can be avoided.

Distance: 10km (6¼ miles). Total ascent: 1200ft (364m).

Start/car parking: Car park below Murlo hamlet. From Monteroni or Buonconvento on the SS2, or from the SS223 south of Siena (junction is signposted to Fontazzi and Murlo); head for Vescovado then turn to the south for 1¼ miles (2km) to Murlo.

Refreshments: Café/bar in Murlo (probably open only in season). There are no shops.

Maps: Kompass 661, Siena, Chianti, Colline Senesi, 1:50 000 (part). Multigraphic, Val d'Orcia, 1:25 000 (part).

The Walk

Leave the car park along the surfaced road to the left. Turn right at the signposted road junction, towards Buonconvento. Despite appearances, this is a quiet minor road with reasonable walking verges. Go steadily uphill for about 1¾ miles (3km). *(About half-way along this stretch of road, after a right hand bend, there is a rough track to the right with a sign to discourage walkers. The far end of this track rejoins the main route close to the shrine. Whether or not to risk a possible reprimand by using this alternative is a matter for personal judgement).*

1. Turn right, uphill, along an unsurfaced road signposted 'Montepertuso', passing a red and white waymark. Ignore possible turnings and pass the little shrine of S. Biagio. *(The alternative track joins from the right in a few metres).* The wide track continues through a comparatively barren landscape, largely scrub and juniper, soon passing a large abandoned house then an overgrown pond. Continue along a broad ridge. Pass a farm pond; *from this area there are views back to Murlo.* As the vegetation becomes more sumptuous, reach a disused quarry, with two former lime kilns *(fornaci),* restored in 1998. At a major fork in a further 200 metres or so keep right, soon joining another track, still bearing right. There are extensive hill views ahead as the track descends.

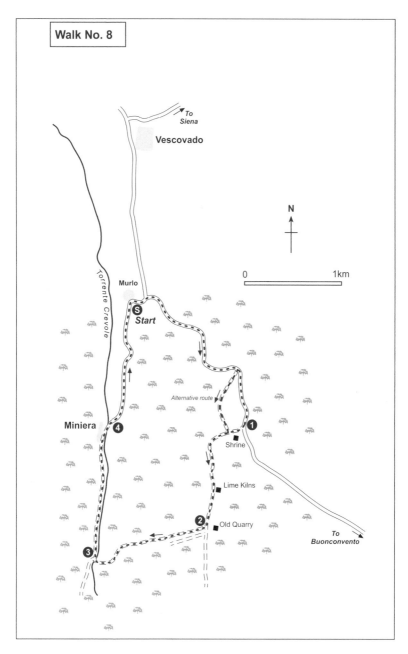

Walk No. 8

To Siena

Vescovado

N

0   1km

Torrente Crevole

Murlo

S *Start*

Alternative route

Miniera **4**

1

Shrine

Lime Kilns

2 Old Quarry

3

To Buonconvento

2. Opposite a disused quarry take the first of two right turns which are close together, to commence the steep descent of the valley side on a broad track. Reach a 'T' junction at the bottom with a wide cultivated field in front. Turn left; the path

47

Murlo

is somewhat overgrown and it may be necessary to walk along the edge of the field to reach and then to cross the shallow stream, the Torrente Crevole, which presents no problem. Follow a good track ascending the far bank to join an unsurfaced roadway by the entrance to a designated nature trail.

3. Turn right, away from the designated trail, to follow the roadway along the line of the former railway for an easy stroll to Miniera, where there are still a few obvious industrial remains. *Most of this former coal-mining village has been renovated and has been given a new lease of life, including a tarmac-surfaced access road.*

4. Bear right at the far end of the village for the quite strenuous ascent back to Murlo.

Places of interest

An important centre in Etruscan times, today Murlo is a sleepy little hamlet close clustered on its knoll. An excavation revealing an Etruscan tomb is situated at the rear of the car park.

Miniera is a former coal-mining village, with an industrial museum and some other obvious remains of that industry. Nearby Buonconvento has a medieval centre with some surviving defensive wall. The newer part of the town is quite nondescript.

Other walks

Walks 6 and 9 are not far away.

'Walking the Val d'Orcia' – booklet published by the Provincia di Siena. Available from tourist information offices.

9. San Giovanni d'Asso

A most attractive circuit over high ground in the very distinctive 'crete', landscape. The largely open countryside is fine for long views but rather short on shade. Walking surfaces are first rate throughout; there are two considerable ascents but neither is formidably steep. There is the opportunity to add an out-and-back extension to Chiusure and the great abbey of Monte Oliveto Maggiore to this walk.

Distance: 7.5km (4¾ miles) – the suggested extension adds 10km (6¼ miles). Total ascent: 650ft (197m) – the suggested extension adds 450ft (136m).

Start/car parking: Substantial free car park by the castle in the centre of San Giovanni. San Giovanni stands on the SS451, approximately 9 miles (14km) south of Asciano and 10 miles (16km) north of San Quirico.

Refreshments: Café in San Giovanni.

Map: Kompass 661, Siena Chianti Colline Senesi, 1:50 000.

The Walk

From the car park walk downhill along the Via Roma, pass a junction with a tree in the middle of the road, reaching a junction with the main road. Turn right to head south-west, following a 'Siena' signpost, along the roadside for almost 800 metres. Cross a stream and continue for 250 metres.

1. At a junction with waymark and other signs, turn right into an unsurfaced roadway signposted 'Ferrano', rising almost at once along an avenue of trees. Stay with this roadway, passing a wayside cross and viewpoint after a right hand bend. Continue to the Villa Ferrano, passing two old wells, then go straight on through lovely rolling countryside, passing the occasional dwelling. Stay with route 555 at a marked junction and carry on through a tiny hamlet. *The views extend as far as the distant Monte Amiata.*

2. Keep right, on route 555 at the next junction, go straight on at another junction, now with views over a different area of countryside, and reach Il Poderino, a considerable Agriturismo. Pass the gate, ascending to the left with views now including the abbey of Monte Oliveto Maggiore, nestling among the trees, and the hilltop village of Chiusure.

49

San Giovanni d'Asso

3. Reach a major junction, with metal gates on the right and a notice concerning livestock.

4. *For Chiusure and the abbey go straight on, soon bearing left across the hillside and follow the well defined trail rising to Chiusure. Turn left at the road and keep to the outside edge of the village until a track leading to the abbey is reached. Turn left here to descend along a path which winds its way directly to the abbey. Unless, of course, there is a non-walking driver or a two-car situation, return by the same route.* The basic route turns right, through the gates, well signposted, along a farm track. *Over a crest, San Giovanni is in view.*

5. At a fork, go right, through another metal gate, again taking note of the advice about livestock. Pass a waymark on a tree then a large farm on the left. The unsurfaced roadway winds

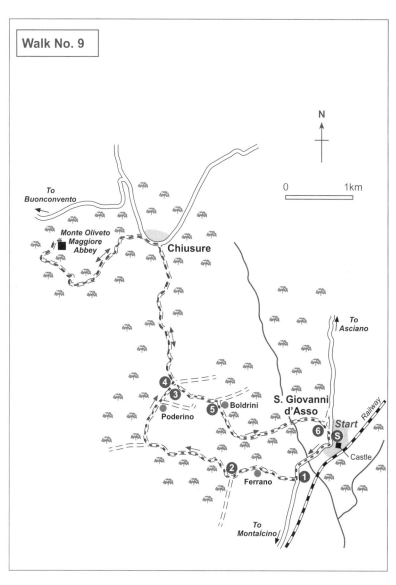

Walk No. 9

round to the left below a hill and San Giovanni comes into view again. Pass a house with waymark and descend to cross a valley. Cross the stream and rise up the far side.

6. At a left hairpin bend on the fringe of the town, go straight on along a gravel roadway, heading for the castle. Join a surfaced road below the castle, turning left to rise to the car parking area.

Places of interest

San Giovanni d'Asso is a large village with shops and other facilities, dominated by a sizeable castle.

Chiusure is a brick-built village of some charm, perched high above typical 'Crete' countryside – deep ravines of greyish clay, sometimes wooded but often bare. The views from Chiusure over this countryside are splendid.

The Abbazia of Monte Oliveto Maggiore was founded early in the 14th century by Bernardo Tolomei and a group of devout friends from Siena who retired to this remote site to live in accordance with the rule of St Benedict. The brickwork buildings were erected in stages, over a long period of time, as the abbey flourished as a centre of spiritual and cultural life. Parts of the complex are open to visitors. Of particular note is the cloister, flanked by 35 scenes from the life of St Benedict, the majority beautifully painted by Sodoma. Inside the early 15th-century church are particularly beautiful choir stalls. Visitor facilities include an information office and a shop selling products made by the monks.

Other walks

Nearest is Walk 8.

Route no. 5 on the 'Provincia di Siena grandi sentieri' map (tourist information offices) links San Giovanni with Trequanda (to the north-east).

10. Orgia

A circuit in the wooded hill country a few miles south of Siena, based on the tiny village of Orgia. The area was a centre of woodland industries such as charcoal burning and Orgia is now home to a museum of wood-based crafts; opening hours for public access are very limited. Walking trails are well organised in this now protected woodland, with numbered routes criss-crossing the hills. The chosen circuit includes a re-creation of a charcoal burner's stack and nearby cabin. There is one quite prolonged ascent near the start.

Distance: 6.5km (4 miles). Total ascent: 625ft (190m).

Start/car parking: By the roadside just short of the main part of Orgia village, opposite the wood museum laboratory building (this is not the museum itself). Leave the Siena to Grosetto main road, SS223, at a turning about 9 miles (14km) south of Siena, signposted to Orgia. In 800 metres turn left, cross the R. Merse and climb the hillside to reach Orgia, keeping right at a fork a little way before the village.

Refreshments: Bar/restaurant 'Cateni' in Orgia.

Map: Kompass 661, Siena, Chianti, Colline Senesi, 1:50 000.

The Walk

Walk uphill to the main part of the village, pass the 'Cateni', turn left then right to leave the village along the Via di Sotto; the road soon becomes a good walking track. Reach the edge of woodland in a short distance, where a notice board sets out the routes of the trails numbered by the Italian Alpine Club. At the adjacent fork take the route to the left, a broad, unsurfaced track rising steadily to a multi junction with several Alpine Club signs.

1. Turn sharp left to follow route 404, soon passing an information board with details of local flora and fauna, including porcupines, wild boar, squirrels, hedgehogs, foxes and woodpeckers. Pass another board with the route map. At a fork go left for 'le carbonaire', level for a short distance before a further rise. Keep right at a waymarked fork, uphill. Pass a four-legged wooden structure and join a more major track.

2. Turn sharp left to reach the replica of the charcoal burn. Retrace your steps for 80 metres and go straight ahead to find the reconstructed charcoal burner's cabin. Carry on, rising gently, a little to the south of west. Join an unsurfaced road-

Charcoal burning at Orgia

way, now route 403, turning left towards 'Romitorio'. Stay with this roadway, ignoring tracks to the left; there is a fence on the right. After passing a substantial property the roadway bends to the right. Pass another flora and fauna board and arrive at the former chapel 'Romitorio'.

3. In 30 metres fork left, pass a pond on the right and go downhill to a major junction.

4. Turn sharp right to follow route 402, signposted 'Orgia', passing the ruin of a stone cabin on the left. Go round the head of a valley, with glimpses of the village of Brenna through the trees on the left. Go straight on at two successive junctions as 402 heads reassuringly towards Orgia, with Montestigliano in view. Descend to the major junction at point 1. on the outward route. Bear to the left to stay with the major track; *Orgia is now in view*. Pass the original route board and continue through the village to the parking place.

Places of interest

Less than 10 miles (16km) from Orgia is the great city of Siena, great not in size but in its importance in the world of art and architecture. In a predominantly walking book, space does not allow justice to be done in attempting to describe the manifest attractions of this marvellous place. Any visitor to Siena should at least find time to savour the atmosphere of the Piazza del Campo, one of the world's great city centre open spaces, and to visit the Duoma, the Pinacoteca Nazionale, the Palazzo Publico as a minimum.

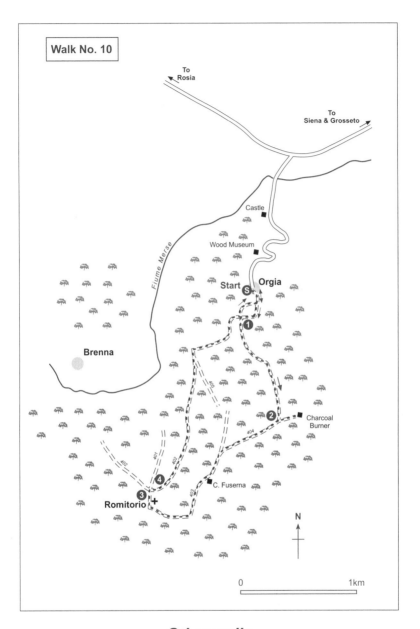

Other walks

Walks 11 and 12 are both close to Orgia.

Other routes can be made from permutations of the numbered trails in the forest above Orgia.

11. Brenna and Torri

A good walk across the hilly wooded countryside linking the villages of Brenna and Torri, using designated and waymarked routes, generally broad easy woodland tracks. The route is part out-and-back and part circuit. The last part of the return route is, however, a steeply descending narrow path which some walkers will not enjoy. An alternative to this path is offered.

Distance: 10km (6¼ miles). Total ascent: 850ft (258m).

Start/car parking: Brenna – informal area at the far end of the village, close to the café/bar. Brenna is reached by leaving the SS223, Siena to Grosseto road at the 'Orgia' junction. Turn left for Brenna in about one mile.

Refreshment: Bar/café at Brenna (top end of village).

Map: Kompass 661, Siena, Chianti, Colline Senesi, 1:50 000.

The Walk

Leave Brenna along a broad track designated 402, passing an isolated church with a sentinel cypress. At a 'T' junction turn right, uphill. There is an Alto Merse Regional Park notice and a waymark. The River Merse is below on the left, with a former mill leat even closer. Join an unsurfaced roadway close to an informal parking area, turning right, uphill. *In spring this area is rich in wild violets.* Pass a junction and bear right, still uphill. Continue, now on route 405(b), rising gently to another junction, where 405 bis joins our route.

1. At a subsequent junction of many tracks, go left then right, with a good view of Poggio hamlet, passing a large swampy depression with a small pond before reaching the 'English village' – Palazzo Stigliano. Descend the lane past the property, turning left at the 'T' junction at the bottom to continue into the little square of Stigliano. *The (seasonal?) café/bar is to the left.*

2. Keep to the right to pass the telephone box and, in 40 metres, look carefully for a little path on the right, over grass, soon descending a few steps to reach a concrete footbridge across a dry stream bed. Ascend the far side to a steep little bank and join a tarmac road by a disused quarry. Go straight on as the tarmac ends and then slightly to the right at a fork. *Oaks and chestnuts line the way.* At a small clearing in 300 metres fork

56

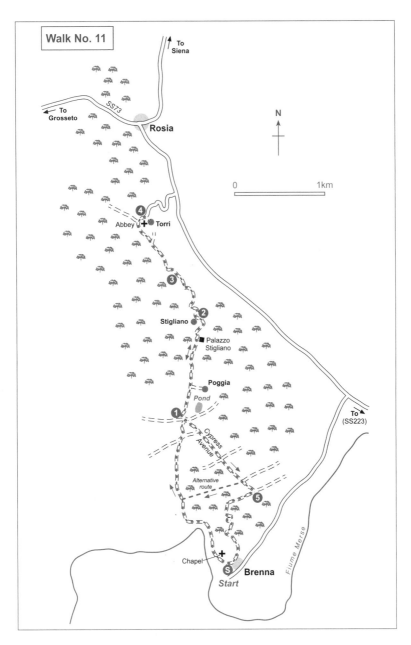

left, uphill, to a meeting place of tracks, defined by four large oak trees.

3. Head between these trees to a narrower path descending between the bramble. Pass a water supply station on the right

Stigliano

and continue uphill. *Torri is now in view through the trees ahead, with Rosia beyond.* Ignore a track descending to the right and stay with the main track, now with cypresses on the right. At a major fork in 120 metres, go left, uphill, the track resplendent with wild crocuses in early spring. The track curves to cross a small dry valley. Ignore tracks to right and left and carry on round the hillside above Torri. Pass a bricked up cave and above the village; the track soon bends abruptly to the right to descend past allotments to join an unsurfaced roadway. Turn right and then right again at the public road to head for an entrance gate to the village. *The abbey entrance is tucked away to the right.*

4. Return by the same route to the junction at point 1, the foot of an avenue of cypresses.

   Ascend between the trees, straight mainly uphill for just over a kilometre, passing two major junctions featuring former mill stones. *This avenue provides a good test of walking speeds: 15 minutes = 3 mph is quite good when going uphill.*

5. At the far end, meet a minor lane and turn right to walk along to substantial derelict buildings. Turn left by the buildings to take a narrow waymarked path into woodland. There are plenty of waymarks as the path weaves around through the trees, which include many oaks. The so far gentle descent steepens considerably after leaving the woodland and the combination of reddish earth with both loose and solid stone does need care. No

walker familiar with, for example, Lake District or Snowdonia hill paths will be inconvenienced as the path drops abruptly to hen pens on the fringe of Brenna. Reach a house drive and zig zag downhill before bearing right to the front of the church. Go down the church steps and turn right then left to reach the road below the village, close to the café/bar and the car park. *(To avoid the steep path, turn right at the second of the two clearings in the long avenue, initially along another wide avenue, descending gently. At a fork, keep right as the track narrows to become a woodland path, a touch overgrown in places but the route is never in doubt. Join a more important track close to a waymark and turn left for a straightforward and pleasant stroll above the River Merse to Brenna, re-using the first part of the outward route.)*

Places of interest

Brenna is an unpretentious but very pleasant old village close to the R. Merse, which formerly provided power for substantial water mills. A small grocery shop and a bar/café are present day assets.

Torri is an ancient little village where the houses face inwards in a close huddle, their backs forming a defensive perimeter wall. Tucked away at the top of the village is a small former abbey with a fine little cloister, open to the public on Mondays and Fridays, only until noon.

Other walks

Walks 10 and 12 are quite close.

See Walk 10 for permutations of numbered woodland walks.

12. Tegoia

The rolling wooded hills to the south-west of Siena extend for many miles towards Grosseto and Maremma. Tegoia provides the focal point for a pleasant little circuit at quite a high level in these hills, with comparatively little up and down. The route uses excellent numbered tracks, unsurfaced roads and footpaths; the waymarking is first class.

Distance: 5km (3 miles). Total ascent: 400ft (121m).

Start/car parking: There is very little space by the roadside in Tegoia. By the public telephone is best. Even better is an off-road informal area 100 metres before the village boundary sign. To access Tegoia, drive along the SS73, Siena to Grosetto road. From Siena direction, turn right about 2 miles before reaching Rosia, signposted 'Sovicille', turn left then left again just before the centre of Sovicille. Turn right in a short distance to commence a long climb up a wooded hillside, turning left at a 'Tegoia' signposted junction in less than 800 metres. From the opposite direction, leave the SS73 at a left turn a little less than one mile after Rosia, then turn left just before the centre of Sovicille to commence the climb mentioned above.

Refreshments: La Montagnola bar/restaurant in Tegoia (closed on Mondays).

Map: Kompass 661, Siena, Chianti, Colline Senesi, 1:50 000.

The Walk

Go through Tegoia and past the restaurant; the road (Siena trail no.114) soon loses its surface. There is a red and white waymark on the right, then long views, including Sovicille village. *Wild flowers in early spring include crocus and primroses. The woodland is predominantly chestnut.* Pass a small memorial on the left. Route 120 joins from the right. Go straight ahead, now following routes 114 and 120 combined.

1. At a junction with several tracks, stay with the unsurfaced road, rising to the right to head for Molli hamlet, passing a derelict farm. At a well-waymarked junction, route 111 joins from the right. *At a fork in 50 metres, the track on the right leads to Molli church.* Dip down to the left, along tracks 116/117 combined.

2. At a junction of several tracks fork left along 117, gently downhill. Keep right at a fork in 400 metres. At the next fork follow

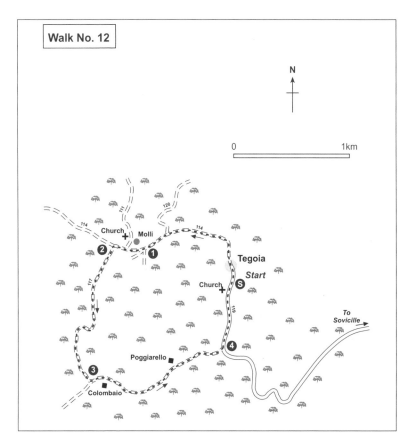

Walk No. 12

the waymark to the right, downhill, now a little rough underfoot. A track joins from the right; go straight ahead along a
lovely woodland path.

3. Join an unsurfaced roadway, with Colombaio Farm in view
   ahead. Turn left to follow this roadway for about 1 mile
   (1.6km), soon passing the large Podere Poggiarello on the left.
   Ignore any track to right or left.

4. Reach the tarmac access road to Tregoia and turn left, uphill,
   to return to the village.

Places of interest

The diminutive town of Sovicille is the undisputed centre of this
area, with a few shops, the municipal administration for quite a
wide area and an up-market restaurant. The old portion of the
town clusters round a square at the top, above a rather faded looking former castle, converted into a spacious villa.

Tegoia is a tiny village with church and bar/restaurant. Siena is only a few miles to the north-east.

Other walks

Walks 10, 11, 13 are all close.

The wooded hills north and west of Sovicille have a large number of excellent trails, numbered and waymarked by the Province of Siena. The possible permutations to form circuits are almost unlimited.

The Animals of Tuscany

By the coast the lagoons harbour flamingos, cormorants, marsh harriers and scores of less flamboyant waterfowl, whilst in the mountains golden eagles, choughs and eagle owls can be seen. Inland lakes have herons, little bitterns and a variety of ducks. On the ground the celebrated wild boar, crested porcupines and mouflons are widespread (although rarely seen by walkers), in more recent years joined by the wolf, which has reappeared in wilder, more mountainous parts. Foxes, badgers, deer, marmots, lizards and snakes are among the more common animals.

For information/booklets: Regione Toscana, Dipartimento delle Politiche Territoriale e Ambientali, via di Novoli, 50100, Firenze, Italy. www.regione.toscana.it

Volpaia: a former castle

North/Central

13. Monteriggioni

A varied circuit focused on the tiny hill town of Monteriggioni, through woodland and open countryside. Underfoot, unsurfaced roadways and a section of narrow woodland path are good and are not difficult to follow, largely due to the above average waymarking. Plenty of ascent on the outward half, but the gradients are never really severe. The return is predominantly downhill to the former abbey of S. Salvatore, followed by a rare area of flat farmland

Distance: 10.5km (6½ miles). Total ascent: 1020ft (309m).

Start/car parking: Large unsurfaced free car park a little way below the walls of Monteriggioni. A smaller car park closer to the town walls requires payment in high season. Monteriggioni is accessed from the main Florence – Siena dual carriageway road. Exit for 'Monteriggioni', a few miles north of Siena then follow the signs for less than 1 mile.

Refreshments: Choice of bars/cafés/restaurants in Monteriggioni.

Map: Kompass sheet 661, Siena, Chianti, Colline Senesi, 1:50 000.

The Walk

Walk back for about 250 metres along the car park access road to join the public road. Turn left, then turn right in 40 metres to follow an unsurfaced roadway signposted 'Strada del Gallinaio'. There is also a notice board and a red and white waymark. Keep right at a fork as the roadway rises gently past vineyards and olive groves.

1. At a junction on a tight left bend stay with the main track and go straight ahead at a crossroads in a further 100 metres. Continue through mixed woodland, passing Gallinaio and soon approaching Ebbio, a substantial property. Ahead is the wooded hillside, which is our next objective. Our route (102 at this point) is confirmed by a waymark on an electricity post.

2. In 200 metres fork left, uphill, along a clear woodland path. At a waymarked junction turn left along a more minor path. The path becomes narrower, quite a contrast to the earlier tracks, but is positive, with confirmation by good waymarking. We are climbing the side of Monte Maggio (671m – 2,202ft). At a waymarked junction turn right, rising through an area of

64

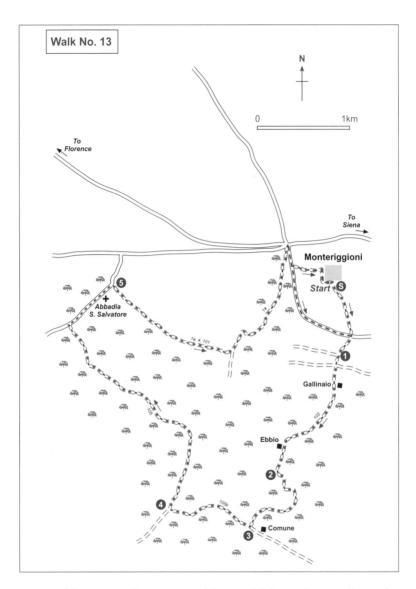

Walk No. 13

To Florence

To Siena

Monteriggioni

Start

Abbadia S. Salvatore

Gallinaio

Ebbio

Comune

scrubby vegetation, soon with an old boundary wall on the right. Go straight on at an apparent junction, with an olive grove on the right and the wall now on the left. Stay with the main track, bearing up to the right at a waymarked junction. *There are glimpses of Monteriggioni through the trees on the right.*

3. Reach an unsurfaced roadway with a waymark and a 105b sign. *To the left is an isolated dwelling.* Turn right, downhill,

passing a large property (no.13) and continue, high along the valley side before starting the long descent. Go straight on at a junction, downhill.

4. At a waymarked 'T' junction in a further 40 metres turn right to continue the descent for almost two miles (3km) along an unsurfaced roadway, passing a touching memorial to 19 (presumably local) men shot by the fascists in March 1944. At the bottom pass a farm with neat buildings, go round to the right at a junction and into a hamlet with a curious hexagonal building – the *'Oratorio della Madonna della Neve' – erected in memory of a miraculous snowfall in Rome in August during the fourth century. This snowfall outlined the plan of a church which the then pope was planning to build. The oratorio later became a private property, losing its religious functions.* Turn right at the main road to walk to the abbey. After the abbey, continue along the roadside for 200 yds.

5. Turn right along the Strada di Valmaggiore, an unsurfaced roadway, soon passing a large property. The route is flat and straight for almost a mile before a welcome bend is reached. Pass a farm and continue along an earth track to reach the edge of a low wooded hill. At a 'T' junction turn left along a pleasant track initially rising gently along the bottom edge of the woodland. Pass a few houses and join the public road. Turn right for 40 metres to a junction. Turn right again, with Monteriggioni now in view, above. In 200 metres turn left into a roadway with a 'no entry' sign for a stiff little ascent to the town. Enter the town through a gateway and go straight through to the gateway at the far side. Go downhill along a surfaced road until the car park is evident below. Turn left down the broad track to the car park. (*As an alternative finish to the walk, avoiding the sharp climb to the town, stay with the public road until the vehicular route to the car park is reached. Turn left to finish. A further option is to turn right before entering the town and to follow an earth track which stays outside the walls before joining the surfaced road above the car park. Turn right to return.*)

Places of interest

Monteriggioni is an incredible survival from medieval times, fully fortified with its continuous wall reinforced by numerous towers. There are only two access gateways. Inside the wall, a considerable piazza is surrounded by church, bars/cafés and shops, all housed in attractive old buildings.

The abbey of San Salvatore offers little for visitors. Built by the

Monteriggioni

Cistercians in 1101, the stark Romanesque structure is tightly hemmed in by other buildings; the cloisters appear to be in a sorry state. The alternative title of 'Isola' refers to the original situation of the abbey as an island in the then extensive marshes.

Other walks

The Province of Siena numbered trails in the wooded hills to the west of Monteriggioni offer a variety of circuits.

14. Radda in Chianti

An excellent Chianti circuit based on the fine little town of Radda, one of the foremost centres of the Chianti Classico wine country. As usual in Chianti, vines, olives and woodland make up a high proportion of the generally hilly landscape. In this case, excellent broad tracks are preceded by an unavoidable start along the roadside.

Distance: 8km (5 miles). Total ascent: 740ft (224m).

Start/car parking: Car park behind the town centre. From the south, turn left after passing along the edge of the old (traffic restricted) town.

Refreshments: Plenty of choice in Radda.

Map: Kompass 660, Firenze – Chianti, 1:50 000. The tourist information centre in the middle of the town has map photocopies (black and white) at 1:25 000 which include this area (but only part of the actual route).

The Walk

Walk back towards the main road; there are small public gardens on the left. Turn left at the main road, facing the cinema, and continue downhill by the roadside. The signposting is for Firenze. *The country views compensate to some extent for the roadside walking.* At the junction at the bottom of the hill, cross the bridge and bear right, along a road signposted to Gaiole. Pass a petrol filling station and reach the Villa Miranda, a hotel/restaurant with wine sales.

1. Turn right at once to descend, initially on tarmac. After crossing a stream start to rise, now on an unsurfaced roadway. Keep right at an apparent fork, with a red and white waymark on a tree, by the entrance to a house. Rise steeply, passing La Torre (tower) to the right, traversing light (largely oak) woodland. By a waymark on a tree keep left, along a lesser track, still rising. *Radda can be glimpsed through the trees.*

   At the top of the rise the excellent track continues through an area of large boulders and light woodland. Pass a wayside cross; *the higher hills to the left are the Monti del Chianti.* Go straight ahead at a waymarked junction, now gently downhill. At a major, signposted, junction bear right along a broad unsurfaced roadway descending gently past Vallimaggio. Join another unsurfaced road and carry on downhill to meet the public road.

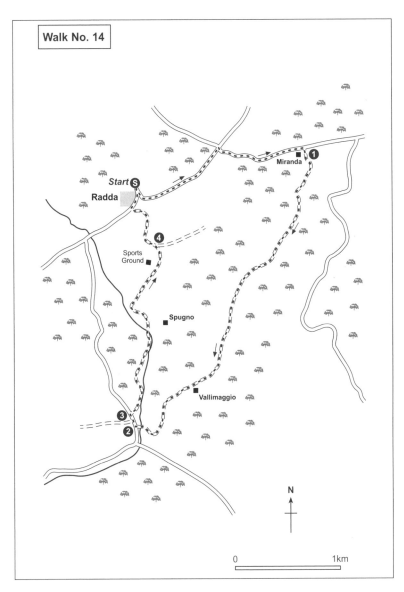

2. Turn right, towards Radda, soon passing a junction with a road to the left.

3. In a further 50 metres, leave the road to turn right into a good track along the side of a valley, initially with a stream burbling happily below on the right, a very welcome sound in Tuscany. There are occasional red and white waymarks to confirm the route. Cross the stream, keep to the main track at any junction,

pass a cliff of crumbling rock and the end of the track leading to Spugno. Pass a farmhouse, rise steeply to pass a house –'Il Duro' and reach the fringe of modern Radda by the football field *(public conveniences here)*.

4. At a 'T' junction turn left for a steady rise along an avenue of pines to join the main road. Turn right, then left at the Piazza 4th November to return to the car park.

Places of interest

Radda is a tightly clustered relic of the middle ages, with much of its great surrounding wall still standing. Included in the Florentine Republic from 1203, Radda was the headquarters of the Chianti League from 1415. The 14th-century parish church of S. Nicolo

Radda: main piazza and church

has a fine fresco on its façade and the adjacent 15th-century Palazzo Pretorio has coats of arms, a good arcade and an ancient clock. It is now the centre of the municipal administration.

Castellina in Chianti is another fine old wine town, a few miles to the west of Radda.

Other walks

All the other walks in the heart of Chianti – Walks 15, 16, 17 and 18 – are within easy distance of Radda.

The Florence to Siena long distance trail (00 waymarks) passes a few miles to the east of Radda.

15. Castello di Brolio

A pleasant little Chianti walk which includes the well-known Brolio Castle within the circuit. Underfoot the route is entirely civilised and there are fine views, particularly of the castle itself. There are no steep gradients and the ascent is comparatively little.

Distance: 5.3km (3 miles). Total ascent: 460ft (140m).

Start/car parking: Castle Brolio is at the heart of the southern part of Chianti, approximately 7 miles (11km) south of the little town of Gaiole in Chianti, from which it is reached via SS484. Approaching from the south use the same road, SS484, via Castelnuovo Berardenga. Close to the massive pillars at the foot of the castle entrance drive, turn down a minor road signposted 'S. Regolo'. Pass through that village and park in an off-road area at a junction in less than 1 mile.

Refreshments: Comprehensive 'osteria' refreshment area below castle (seasonal). Bar and café in S. Regolo.

Map: Kompass 661, Siena . Chianti . Colline Senesi, 1:50 000.

The Walk

Start uphill along the roughish roadway which joins the S. Regolo road at the parking area, through light woodland then passing a large cultivated field, with first glimpses of the castle through the trees on the left. To the right is a huge vineyard and a hilltop farmstead. *The castle is soon in full view.* Continue to a junction close to another large wine property, La Grotta.

1. Join the Chianti Way (OO waymark), turning left to follow 'Castel Brolio' and other signs. Carry on along a good roadway, rising quite steeply initially; views include a fair proportion of the Classico wine area.

2. Reach a corner of the castle wall and continue down the access drive. *Alternatively, walk beside the castle wall as far as the entrance gate – essential if a visit to the castle itself is to be combined with the walk. Continue to the top of a nearby flight of steps. Descend and go down a steep cobbled footpath to rejoin the access drive.* The drive, an avenue of cypresses, makes a good route as it descends in a series of tight bends. Pass the Osteria del Castello, with a large car park opposite, and then go through the gate pillars to join the public road.

3. In 50 metres, turn left, close to a huge modern winery, along the minor road signposted 'S. Regolo'. Follow this minor road past a *lavatoria* (public washing place) to the village, with its trim little church and small bar/grocery shop and café opposite. Carry on down a 25% gradient, passing olive groves and a little cemetery on the return to the parking area.

Places of interest

Brolio Castle is a visitor attraction, claimed to be open to the public virtually every day, from 9 a.m. to noon and from 3 p.m. to 7 p.m. (6 p.m. on Sundays). However, the castle may occasionally be found to be closed and, out of season, opening after darkness obviously cannot be expected. To obtain entry pull the rope on the left of the entrance, which rings a bell. The custodian then operates a remote device which unlocks the metal gates. To leave the castle, press a switch on the right of the gateway. Because of its strategic position, the mighty castle was active from the 13th century in the prolonged frontier wars between Florence and Siena.

Badly damaged by the Sienese in 1529, it was extensively rebuilt later in that century. From the start, the history of the castle has been closely linked to the Ricasoli family, noble overlords of much of the area. In the mid 19th century, Bettino Ricasoli laid the foundations of the distinctive Chianti wine industry by his careful blending of grapes to produce the consistent quality which has since become widely established. Despite the development of an adjacent modern winery, fine wine still matures in the ancient cel-

Brolio Castle garden

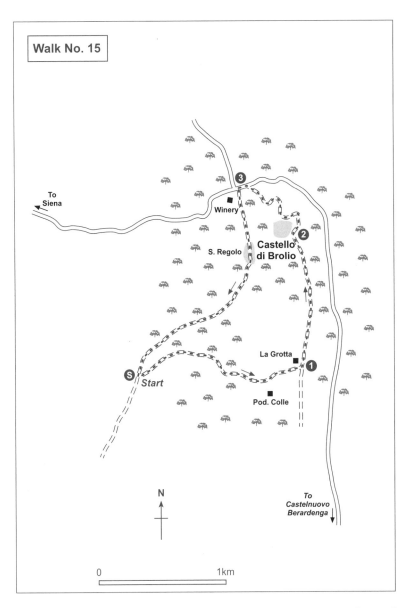

Walk No. 15

To Siena

Winery

❸

S. Regolo

Castello di Brolio

❷

La Grotta

❶

❺ Start

Pod. Colle

N

To Castelnuovo Berardenga

0   1km

lars. At the same time, he transformed the fortress into the red brick Neo Gothic castle seen today. Generally, the public visit is restricted to the church, the gardens and the tops of the walls, from which the views are long and wide.

Gaiole in Chianti is the nearest town, one of the handful which act as focal points in the Chianti countryside, otherwise a large area dotted with small villages and scattered wine and olive estates. The Romanesque church of Santa Maria e Spaltenna dates from the first half of the 12th century. It has to be said that Gaiole is not the prettiest of these historic towns.

Approximately 9 miles (14km) to the south of Brolio Castle, a pyramid on the hill opposite Montaperti village marks the site of a great battle in the Florence vs. Siena wars, fought in 1260. Against the prevailing odds, the Sienese won an important victory.

Other walks

The Florence to Siena long distance trail (waymark OO) forms the spine of this walk. To north or south, this trail can readily be incorporated with other numbered routes and/or minor roads to form good circuits.

Walk 14.

The Wines of Tuscany

 The best-known wine-producing area of Tuscany has long been Chianti, with its raffia-swathed bottles popular in Britain – pretty, even if the wine was often of indifferent quality. In fact, Chianti is now a good example of the overall improvements mentioned above. The quality of the products of the Chianti Classico heartland is jealously guarded, with the black 'Gallo Nero' cockerel as a proud symbol of these wines, which can be sampled and, of course, purchased at scores of the local vineyards. The wider area using merely the 'Chianti' classification is more diverse, the wines are generally cheaper and, overall, the quality is lower, although there are exceptions.

Also based on the Sangiovese grape, the expensive Brunello, from the Montalcino area, has become the aristocrat of Tuscan red wines. The younger, lighter, Rosso di Montalcino is an attractive cheaper alternative to the Brunello. A few miles further to the east is Montepulciano, where the Vino Nobile is another quality product based on the ubiquitous Sangiovese grape. As with Brunello, there is a cheaper but more variable alternative – Rosso di Montepulciano.

Despite the rise and rise of the Tuscan reds, surprisingly it is white wine which is truly historic in Tuscany and a significant amount is still produced, largely from the traditional but somewhat ordinary Trebbiano grape. More up-to-date vineyards are growing Chardonnay and Sauvignon varieties to produce modern style wines. Names to look out for are the Verneccia of the San Gimignano area and the delicate, crisp, Pitigliano in the south of the region.

16. Volpaia

Another opportunity to walk around some of the hilly wine country of Chianti, this time a little way north of the wine town of Radda. The tracks are good and there is less than 800 metres of minor road included in the circuit. The destination of the walk is the church of S. Maria Novella.

Distance: 5.5km (3½ miles). Total ascent: 700ft (212m).

Start/car parking: Car park at entrance to Volpaia. Volpaia is about 5 miles (8km) north of Radda in Chianti, accessed via a minor road. The road junction north-east of Radda requires a right turn then right again through an underpass.

Refreshments: Café/bar in Volpaia.

Map: Kompass 660, Firenze. Chianti, 1:50 000.

The Walk

Walk back down the access road in the direction of Radda for almost 800 metres. *Views of the Chianti countryside are long and wide.*

1. At a sharp right hand bend, there are 3 tracks on the left. Turn down the furthest, at a 'strada privata' sign, a broad earth track descending quite steeply. At a junction by a stone building go straight ahead through the vineyards, soon passing round a solidly built stone house and continuing downhill along the access drive. Pass above a small reservoir on the left, rising gently through oak woodland.

2. Join a more important roadway, turning right, uphill. Cross the Radda to Volpaia road and take the broad, unsurfaced roadway opposite. In a few metres, arrive at a multi junction, where there are route directions on a rock. Bear left, slightly downhill, to cross a small stream before rising to reach a junction, again with directions on rocks.

3. Turn left to head for S. Maria Novella on another broad track through light woodland with patches of bramble. Descend to cross a deep valley, high over the stream at the bottom, cross a tributary stream then bear left to ascend the far side of the valley and reach the public road directly opposite the church of S. Maria Novella. *There is an information board at the far side of the church.* Return across the road and retrace your steps as far as the junction with route directions on rocks (point

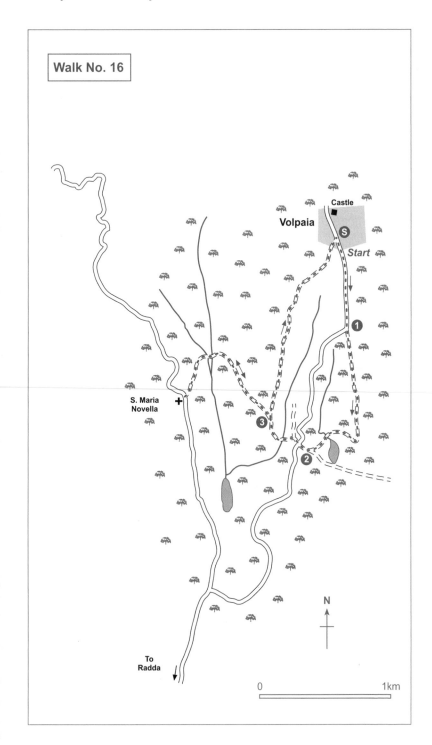

Walk No. 16

Castle

Volpaia

S Start

1

S. Maria
Novella

3

2

N

To
Radda

0   1km

3). Turn left for 'Volpaia', along an unsurfaced roadway, steadily uphill. In 100 metres, pass another 'Volpaia' signposted rock, plodding on to pass an old farmhouse/holiday villa. *S. Maria Novella can be seen through the trees on the left.* Pass another farmstead, keeping to the left of the house. Volpaia is soon in view on its hilltop, ahead. At a signposted junction, turn left. Go straight on at the next junction. Pass a shrine on the left and continue along an avenue of cypresses pointing straight into the village. A lovely little roadway, enclosed by high stone walls is the Viale del Nonno (Grandfather Street). In front of the church you can turn right to return direct to the car park without entering the village proper. *But don't fail to walk round the village!*

Places of interest

The original defensive walls, of local sandstone, surrounding the ancient village of Volpaia were constructed in the 12th/13th centuries. However, early in the 14th century the compact castle within those walls became one of the major centres of the Chianti League, resulting in the construction of an improved surrounding wall, with towers. Part of this wall is still visible. From the 16th century the castle has lost its defensive function. The 14th-century parish church, dedicated to S. Lorenzo, has a sextangular arch. The area inside the walls is small, the close-packed properties being linked by little streets and alleyways. S. Eufrosino church, known as La Commenda, was established in 1443 outside the gate of the castle to shelter and provide care for pilgrims and wayfarers. The structure has characteristics of the early Florentine Renaissance.

The three naves of the previously Romanesqe church of S. Maria Novella were completely rebuilt early in the 19th century. Outside, three columns, with antique capitals, from the original structure, are still visible. Inside, there are frescoes and della Robbia style panels on the font. Unfortunately, the church may be found to be locked.

Radda in Chianti and Greve in Chianti – see walks 14 and 18.

Other walks

Walks 14, 17 and 18 in this book.

Other walks based on Radda – routes available from tourist information office in Radda.

17. Lamole and the Monti del Chianti

A walk in the wooded hills of Chianti's highest area, largely on the flanks of Monte S. Michele, which reaches a height of 892m (2928ft), necessitating a long ascent from the start. Also uphill is the final section along the very quiet Lamole access road. The return track is a little overgrown in places but is not difficult to follow. Otherwise the tracks are excellent.

Distance: 8.7km (5½ miles). Total ascent: 1200ft (364m).

Start/car parking: Area in front of the church in Lamole. From SS222 (the 'Chianti Wine Road') turn to the east a little more than 1 mile south of Greve in Chianti (3 miles – 5km – north of Panzano). The junction is signposted to Lamole. The very minor road twists and turns as it climbs to reach the elevated village in about 5 miles (8km).

Refreshments: Café/bar in Lamole.

Map: Kompass 660, Firenze. Chianti, 1:50 000.

The Walk

At a junction of 3 roadways beyond the church, take the one furthest left, by a board with local walks numbers, and head uphill. In 50 metres, the road loses its surface. There is a red and white waymark on an electricity pole. Join the surfaced road giving access to La Masse hamlet and turn sharp left to continue the ascent.

1. In a short distance turn left into a rising stony track, opposite a house with a stone figure of a dog on a gatepost. The track soon reaches woodland, rising steadily with a communications tower in view on a hilltop to the left. Pass a section of natural rock 'pavement'. At an apparent fork, stay right with the main track. Cross a tiny stream at the head of a valley, bearing left before turning right to ascend more steeply, with a few twists and turns and the occasional waymark. Go left at a waymarked junction and continue to another waymarked junction.

2. Go left again, now rewarded by a stroll along a level section of the route. The next junction is in not much more than 100 metres . Go left yet again and keep left at a fork in 20 metres to rise to a junction. Go straight on to join an earth roadway; there are now long views to the west. Continue, straight on at a junction in a dip, rising again to a multi junction with a small shelter, something of a focal point on this broad hill ridge.

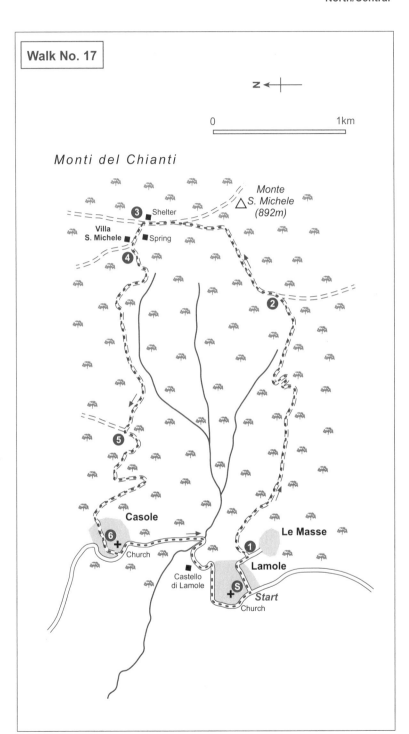

Walk No. 17

N

0   1km

Monti del Chianti

Monte
△ S. Michele
(892m)

❸ Shelter

Villa
S. Michele ■   ■ Spring

❹

❷

❺

Casole

❻ + Church

Le Masse

❶

Lamole

Castello
di Lamole

Ⓢ +
Start
Church

3. Fork left, downhill, by a board displaying numbered walking routes. *Some trees hereabouts have descriptive labels.* In 200 metres, reach a board 'fonte del barbiere'. *A few metres to the left there is a tiny spring, with picnic tables nearby.* Continue along the main track to reach a splendid villa on the right.

4. Opposite the far end of the villa turn left, down a farm track. In 200 metres bear left, downhill, soon reaching a fork. Turn right here – there is a waymark round the corner. Descend steeply, going left at the next junction. Pass waymarks on rocks to carry on straight ahead, downhill on a narrow path, somewhat overgrown and distinctly unpromising – but do have faith! The path soon improves with sections above an old retaining wall and then cobbled – evidently a former mule track. Go straight on at a junction, the track now broad and easy as it passes through light woodland high above a valley bottom.

5. Turn left at a junction with an unsurfaced roadway – a sign here shows our route as '28'. Descend quite steeply, passing an outlying farm, now with fine views. Go round a sweeping left bend and stay with the roadway as it winds its way down the long hillside, passing old stone properties and the occasional waymark. Approach Casole, bearing right to pass behind the buildings. The road becomes surfaced before dropping steeply to the left to join the main road near the church.

6. Turn left to walk along the roadside for rather more than 1 mile, largely uphill, back to Lamole, crossing the stream with an apparent former water mill and passing the substantial old property, Castello di Lamole, on the way.

Castello di Lamole

Olives

Rooted as deeply in Tuscan antiquity as the vine, with which it so often shares a hillside, the olive has been as symbolic as the cypress and the umbrella pine in defining the essential landscape, providing challenges for those seeking to create those meaningful Tuscan pictures which we all so admire.

As an essential ingredient of Mediterranean cuisine, great quantities of olives are produced in Tuscany, in common with other areas of Southern Europe. Historically, every peasant farmer always grew enough olives to cater for at least the needs of his own family. The general agricultural improvements of recent years have merely applied a more businesslike approach to the industry, demonstrated by well-tended groves of trees in a precise pattern, often comprising younger trees. In contrast, some of the ancient groves are still producing good yields, whilst others are choked by undergrowth, presumably with a non-commercial output.

As might be expected, Tuscans regard their olive oil as the best in the world, often carefully hand picked, using nets to avoid bruising the falling fruit. The first pressing, with less than 1% acid content, carries the prestigious 'Extra Virgin' designation, whilst 1%-2% acid content qualifies merely as 'Virgin'.

Places of interest

High on the slopes of the Monti del Chianti, the little village of Lamole has a bar/café, a church and very little else. The church has painted ceilings and oil paintings by masters of the Siena school.

Casole is a hamlet with a church.

The long, broad spine of the Chianti hills forms an attractive area for walkers, as the network of (sometimes confusing) tracks testifies. Monte S. Michele is the highest point.

Greve in Chianti and Radda in Chianti – see walks 18 and 14.

Other walks

In an area criss-crossed with numbered routes, most noteworthy is the Florence to Siena long-distance path, a high level trail of about 47 miles (75km), keeping closely to the spine of the Chianti hills. Starting at San Donato in Collina in the north, the trail finishes at Due Ponti, outside Siena. The 00 waymark is used throughout. Allow 4 or 5 days for the complete route. Details from tourist information offices.

18. Greve in Chianti

An entirely typical Chianti walk – up and down with vineyards, olive groves and mixed woodland. A short distance along public road, but otherwise using excellent broad tracks.

Distance: 8.7km (5½ miles). Total ascent: 750ft (227m).

Start/car parking: There are several car parks close to the main road (SS 222) through Greve. As good as any is one on the east side of that road, a little to the north of the town centre.

Refreshments: Many bars/cafés in Greve. Those situated in the main piazza are most pleasant for outdoor refreshment.

Map: Kompass 660, Firenze. Chianti, 1:50 000.

The Walk

Walk north by the side of the main road for about 500 metres, passing a music school. The road crosses a stream; walkers have a wooden bridge alongside the road.

1. A few metres past the bridge turn right – there are road signs to Uzzano. Pass through an area of modern housing and go left by a little shrine. In a few metres, turn right, uphill, on a broad track signposted to Uzzano, the road losing its surface at once. Rise steadily past olive groves and isolated houses, with Greve spread out below. The track levels, passing a big house. Rise more gently past a shrine, soon reaching the boundary wall of the splendid Castello di Uzzano, a well-guarded mansion set back on the right. Continue round the property boundary and go downhill along an unsurfaced avenue.

2. At a junction with many signs, bear right to 'Le Caselle', along a private road, a broad track descending through pine woods. Stay with this main track at any junction, soon passing the boundary of a country property. Fork right at once (red, yellow and white waymark), downhill then up again.

3. Reach a junction with signs. Fork right here, downhill, following 'Convertoie'. Stay with the main track at a fork – there are signs on a rock – passing a ruined building. The buildings of Convertoie are now well seen across a deep valley. Look carefully for a map painted on a big rock and fork right immediately to descend the side of the valley on a more minor track. Cross a bridge over the stream and bear right to ascend the far side of the valley. Join another farm track, possibly with some mud

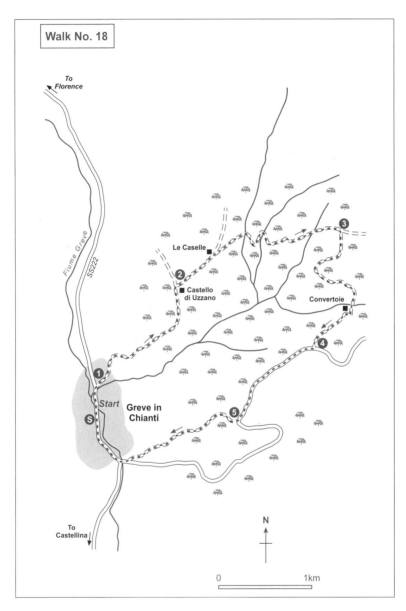

Walk No. 18

To Florence

Fiume Greve

SS222

Le Caselle

2

Castello di Uzzano

Convertoie

3

4

1

Start

Greve in Chianti

S

5

To Castellina

N

0   1km

and bramble, to pass well below the great bulk of Convertoie. The track circles to the right to reach the parking area of the property. Turn left to follow the surfaced access road, quite steeply uphill, to its junction with the public road.

4. Turn right to descend towards Greve. In 800 metres, the road bends sharply to the left by the grounds of a prominent villa.

5. Turn right along an unsurfaced roadway descending attractively past olive groves. Eventually the track becomes hard surfaced, passing dwellings on the fringe of Greve before joining a more important road. Bear right, passing a cinema and a splendid metal sculpture of a black cock, the symbol of the Chianti Classico wine organization. There are public conveniences to the left before the main road is joined. Turn right to return to the recom-

The piazza at Greve

mended car park in a short distance.

Places of interest

Greve is one of three or four small towns which form the heart of Chianti, that alluring wine and olive countryside dear to the hearts of British visitors. As a focal point of the Gallo Nero, Chianti Classico area, its wine credentials are impeccable. An ancient town centre is flanked by extensive residential suburbs and the rather unappealing main street is more than compensated for by the lovely triangular Piazza Matteoti with its arcaded buildings, several being enticing Bars/trattoria. A butcher's shop, Antica Macelleria Falomi has long been famous for wild boar ham and other traditional delicacies. Santa Croce parish church has a noted Madonna and a 15th-century triptych.

Mid September visitors may be delighted to participate in a week long wine festival – the Rassegna del Chianti Classico.

Other wine towns such as Castellina and Radda are likewise of medieval origin and are within easy driving distance of Greve

Badia a Passignano, a Gothic monastery founded in 1049 is less than 4 miles (6km) to the west of Greve. There is a celebrated painting of the 'Last Supper' by Domenico Ghirlandaio, of 1476.

Other walks

Walks 14, 16 and 17 in this book are focused on towns and villages within a few miles of Greve.

19. San Donato

An archetypical 'Tuscan walk', up hill and down dale across rolling countryside with olives, vines, arable fields and a little woodland. Fine views include the showpiece town of San Gimignano, a few miles distant. Entirely good underfoot, with farm tracks and comparatively little public road. San Donato, Montauto, Cuiciano and Ranza are all attractive old hamlets, but without shops or other facilities.

Distance: 8.3km (5¼ miles). Total ascent: 820ft (248m).

Start/car parking: Off-road space for a few vehicles by the refuse storage area at the south entrance from the main road to San Donato hamlet. From San Gimignano head south along the road towards Castel San Gimignano for about 5 miles (8km). From the south the approach is via Colle di Val d'Elsa, heading for Volterra then turning right just before Castel San Gimignano.

Refreshments: None en route.

Map: Multigraphic, S. Gimignano, Volterra, Carta Turistica e dei Sentieri, 1:25 000.

The Walk

Walk through San Donato hamlet, pass the church and take the second turn on the right, a surfaced road with a right turn waymark, signposted to Fattoria Voltrona. The surface is soon lost as the roadway descends steadily in open countryside. Pass a farm and continue to the Fattoria Voltrona, a substantial farm complex.

1. Go round the boundary of the buildings and carry on to a pair of detached dwellings. Pass

Farm near San Donato

between the houses and go steeply downhill, bearing to the left. At the bottom pass well to the left of another house and follow the signpost 'San Gimignano and Montauto'. The track is now over grass. Cross a small boggy area without difficulty and take a track bearing to the left. Turn right at a waymark for a steep ascent between rows of vines.

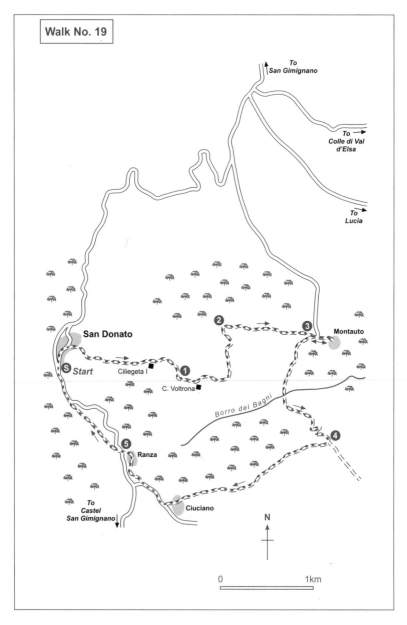

Walk No. 19

To
San Gimignano

To →
Colle di Val
d'Elsa

To →
Lucia

San Donato

② ③ Montauto

S *Start* Ciliegeta I ①

C. Voltrona ■

Borro dei Bagni

④

⑤ Ranza

To
Castel
San Gimignano

Ciuciano

N

0   1km

2. Turn right at the top to head for a modern brick house. Pass in front of the house and continue along an unsurfaced road. After passing another property the church at Montauto, ahead, can just be seen.

3. Just before reaching the tarmac road at Montauto turn sharp

right into an unsurfaced roadway signposted 'Fattoria il Piano'. *To visit Montauto make a short diversion from the circuit at this point.* The roadway descends the valley side. Cross the Borro dei Bagni stream and ascend the far side of the valley along a most attractive and typically Tuscan avenue of cypresses. *The rise is rather more than 300ft (91m) and the shade is very welcome on a hot day.* The Fattoria stands at the top of the rise.

4. Just short of the buildings turn right along a track signposted to Ciuciano, into woodland, soon passing a metal cross on a brick plinth and across the top of an apparently man-made cave. Continue to rise gently along a broad ridge with splendid views and a huge olive grove. Pass a waymark and fork right at a junction, with an old dug-out pond behind a bank on the left. Go straight through Ciuciano hamlet, with the unrenovated authenticity of its very old houses and other buildings proved beyond doubt by widespread tumbledown conditions. Continue quite steeply downhill along the access roadway, with a view of a large prison. As the roadway bends to the left to join the main road, go straight ahead on a track rising to and through Ranza, where there is obvious renovation of several properties.

5. Join the San Gimignano road, going uphill for less than 100 metres. Cross the road and turn left into a fine track rising in parallel with the road. This is an ancient route with the old paved surface still evident. Join a more modern track at the top, initially gravelled, and bear right to join the main road. The parking place is reached in a further 400 metres.

Places of interest

The wonderful hill town of San Gimignano is within sight of part of the above route – see walk no.21 for a brief description.

A little further, to the south-east, Colle di Val d'Elsa has a medieval upper town, within 13th-century walls.

Other walks

Walks 20 and 21 in this book.

20. Volterra

A fine circular walk through the countryside to the north of the marvellous town of Volterra. Like the Duke of York we climb steadily up to the top of the hill, with the inevitable corollary. But the Duke's men would be unlikely to have enjoyed such lovely scenery along the way. The mixture of old mule trails, minor roadways and Volterra town centre is superb.

Distance: 8.5km (5¼ miles). Total ascent: 1150ft (348m).

Start/car parking: By the restaurant/bar 'Prato d'Era' there are roadside spaces. From the direction of Siena/Colle di Val d'Elsa, turn right at Roncolla, approximately 3 miles (5km) short of Volterra, signposted 'Pontedera'. At a junction in about 4 miles (6km) turn left, signposted 'Volterra' and park on the grass verge before the bar/restaurant.

Refreshments: At the Prato d'Era. Selection in Volterra.

Map: Multigraphic, Carta Turistica e dei Sentieri, S. Gimignano, Volterra, 1:25 000.

The Walk

Facing the Prato d'Era restaurant, take the track to the right of the property, commencing the rise which predominates all the way to Volterra. In 150 metres, fork right along a grassy track to continue the ascent, soon passing a well cared for little shrine. Old paving demonstrates former use as a mule track as we rise along the side of a well-wooded valley.

1. At a fork in less than 800 metres keep right, uphill. *Grassy banks are covered in wild flowers.* Pass an agricultural building, still rising, and perhaps reflecting on the sturdiness of the poor old mules which hauled heavy packs up these demanding trails. Pass a water trough on the right, replete with frogs. At a junction above a house follow the cobbles to the right.

2. Join a minor road, turning left to pass olive groves. As the road bends sharp right by a little shrine, fork left along another rising mule track. Keep right at a junction in 100 metres.

3. Rejoin the road and enjoy splendid long views. Turn left, soon passing the turning into the Zona Archeologica. In the bank on the left several preserved Etruscan tombs can be seen. Turn left along a track close to a 'Zona Archeologica' notice. In 30 metres, turn right, uphill. Join a very minor surfaced road,

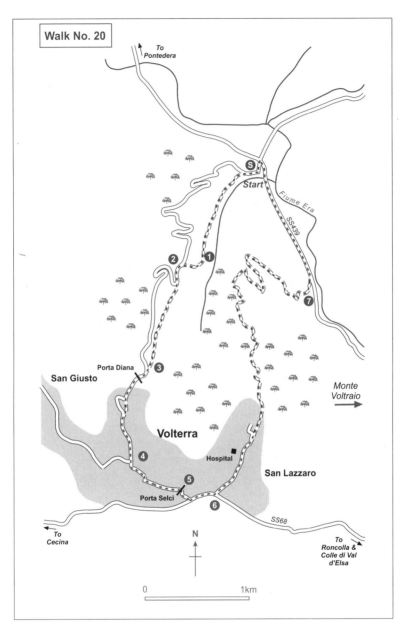

Walk No. 20

To Pontedera

S Start

Fiume Era

SS439

2 1

7

Porta Diana

San Giusto 3

Monte Voltraio →

Volterra

Hospital

4

San Lazzaro

5

Porta Selci

6

SS68

To Cecina

N

To Roncolla & Colle di Val d'Elsa

0   1km

going straight ahead, with Volterra in view on its hill ahead. Join a more important road and pass the remains of the great Porta Diana, with surviving Etruscan stonework. *A little further, on the right, is the entrance to a most remarkable cemetery, with elegant arcaded buildings surrounding the burial*

Medici fortress, Volterra

area. As the road bears right, go straight on, uphill, along the Rampa della Cocina, passing an oratory of 1571.

4. Join another road and go straight ahead to make your triumphal entry to Volterra through the Porta Fiorentina. Continue along the Via Guarnacci to a European University Laboratory. Turn left along the Via di Sotto, pass through the Piazza 20th September, pass the Etruscan Museum and reach the Porta a Selci, beside the superb Medici fortress.

5. Go through the gate to a war memorial, set on a terrace, with seats. Pass the memorial and descend a long flight of steps to the left, carrying on to join the main road. Turn left to walk along the roadside, passing a filling station.

6. Turn left into Via Luigi Scabia, signposted 'Ch. S. Girolamo'. This is a waymarked minor road. Go straight on at a junction, soon reaching S. Girolamo, a former monastery of which a church of unusual design remains. *Through glass at either end of the frontage, Della Robbia altar pieces dated 1501 may be seen.* Pass hospital buildings and continue along the road, soon forking right, downhill. *The long views are excellent; to*

the right the beautifully shaped Monte Voltraio is prominent.
Fork right at a junction, still descending. Pass a neglected cemetery on the right and the occasional house and waymark. After a waymarked right bend continue through more open country to a hairpin bend, then zig zag down the hillside. Pass a house on the left and, in 100 metres, turn very sharp left along a broad, unsurfaced track (waymark on tree). Pass a graveyard for elderly cars then turn sharp right 50 metres after passing another house. At a junction of paths go straight ahead to descend to a quiet public road.

7. Turn left to walk along the roadside for just over a kilometre, along the Era valley, to a junction signposted 'Volterra'. Turn left to return to the car parking area.

Alabaster

Close to Volterra, the extraction of alabaster is of similar antiquity. This soft variety of gypsum, delicately shaded, was ideal for carving into the funery urns beloved of the Etruscans, from the 6th to the 1st centuries BC. After the Roman period, its use faded away until the Renaissance, when wealthy families recognised its value in sculptural decoration. By the mid-19th century many craftsmen were working this attractive stone. Volterra now has a multitude of craft premises and shops offering articles of all shapes and sizes, from simple bowls and ashtrays to complex ornaments.

Places of interest

Volterra is steeped in history. A pre-historic settlement was succeeded by the Etruscan city of Velathri, one of the twelve city states of the Etruscan League. This city covered an area about three times the size of the present town. In the 3rd century BC the Romans took over, establishing the municipality of Volaterrae. In the middle ages it was a free (self governing) commune until brought under Florentine protection in 1361. The abundant historic remains include Etruscan burial chambers, archaeological park, museum and the remains of town walls, a Roman amphitheatre, palaces – the 13th-century Palazzo del Priori is the oldest town hall in Tuscany – a 12th-century cathedral and a Medici fortress. To see the cathedral, the Piazza dei Priori, with its palaces, and the archaeological park, short diversions from the route through Volterra are required.

Other walks

Walks 19 and 21.

Linear walk from Saline di Volterra to the outskirts of Volterra, using the trackbed of the former railway line (uphill – the railway was operated on a rack and pinion system).

21. San Gimignano

It would be difficult to find a more pleasing circuit in the whole of Tuscany. Straightforward walking, largely on unsurfaced roadways, an easy to follow circuit, long views in several directions and, above all, the superb town of San Gimignano on the skyline. Despite considerable rise and fall, the gradients are never excessive. And, last but not least, the walk finishes by traversing the main street of the town, through two piazzas replete with pavement cafés.

Distance: 9km (5½ miles). Total ascent: 820ft (250m).

Start/car parking: As might be expected in a town of such immense visitor attraction, San Gimignano's car parking is diffuse, spread along the outside of the ancient walls. Any of the various car parks will suffice, but for this walk the Parcheggio Bagnaia on the north side of town is particularly convenient. Payment is required; many will no doubt be able to find a free roadside space not too far away. From wherever you park, walk to the northern edge of town, where the main road to the north and west descends away from the town, signposted to, inter alia, Certaldo.

Refreshments: Plenty of choice of bars/cafés in San Gimignano.

Map: Multigraphic, S. Gimignano, Volterra, Carta Turistica e Dei Sentieri, 1:25 000.

The Walk

With your back to San Gimignano set off down the Certaldo road mentioned above. In less than 200 metres, turn sharp right to follow a minor road signposted to Ulignano. There is a red and white waymark on a tree.

1. In less than 800 metres, take the sharper of two right turns, by a tiny church, to continue along an unsurfaced roadway. Follow this roadway for nearly 2¼ miles (3.6km). The route is well waymarked and is never in doubt. *The views are both back to San Gimignano and over great swathes of Tuscan countryside, displaying the subtle blending colours of vines, olives and woodland. Inevitably the vineyards bring to mind the crisp and refreshing Vernaccia, offered in every wine shop for miles around.* Towards the end the roadway rises under trees and there are three caves artificially cut into the soft rock.

San Gimignano

2. At a junction with many signposts leave the roadway by forking right along a lesser track (waymark on tree). In 40 metres, fork right again at another lesser track (waymark at junction), now descending gently. Bear left then right to pass a large house and continue towards San Gimignano before descending steeply to join a main road. Turn right to walk by the roadside for less than 400 metres.

3. Turn right, along a little waymarked roadway, initially tarmac but soon losing its surface. This is another fine track rising inexorably but not too steeply all the way back to San Gimignano, 1½ miles or so. *Again, the views are great and few will resist the opportunity of photographing San Gimignano from this angle.* At the end of this track rise more steeply on tarmac for a short distance before bearing to the right and ascending a flight of steps.

4. Continue through the Porta San Giovanni gateway into town and along the main street, Via San Giovanni. Pass through Piazza della Cisterna and Piazza Duomo and carry on along the Via San Matteo. Fifty metres before reaching the Porta San Matteo gateway, turn right into the Via San Martino; there are signs pointing to the Parcheggio Bagnaia. Continue across a junction to follow another similar signpost to a passageway through the town walls.

5. Turn right along an earth track. In 50 metres, descend a long flight of steps, cross the road and return to the car park. *To*

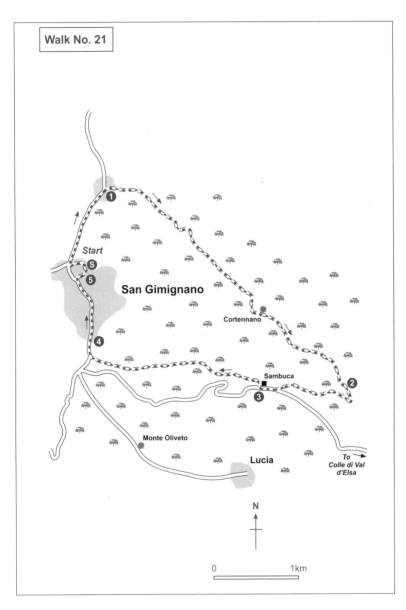

Walk No. 21

Start

San Gimignano

Cortennano

Sambuca

Monte Oliveto

Lucia

To
Colle di Val
d'Elsa

N

0   1km

return to any other car park, take an appropriate route from the
town centre. There are street maps in most of the visitor guide
books; they are also available from the tourist information
centre.

Places of interest

The wonders of San Gimignano occupy several pages in most visitor guides. Regarded by many as Italy's best-preserved medieval town, it is a defensive stronghold and an unforgettable landmark on its hill above the rolling countryside. Most noteworthy are the towers; just 15 of the original 70 or so remain from an era when each important family built a tower to demonstrate power and wealth. The traffic restrictions help in creating a historic time capsule, with lovely streets, churches and other buildings.

Certaldo has a medieval town on a hill, with a larger modern town below.

Other walks

Walks 19 and 20.

The recommended map has several marked and named circular trails based on San Gimignano.

Vagli Sotto (Walk 25)

The North

22. Bagni di Lucca

*A first class hilly walk on the lower flanks of the Appennines.
There is a long sustained ascent early in the circuit, followed by
a shorter ascent a little further on. Thereafter, the route
contours delightfully round a hillside. Underfoot are good paths
and unsurfaced roadways. The widespread views include the
Apuan Alps to the west.*

Distance: 10.5km (6½ miles). Total ascent: 1400ft (424m).

Start/car parking: Parking area beside the church at Bagni
Calda. Drive north-east through Bagni di Lucca on the north
side of the River Lima. Pass a piazza and the Hotel Roma then
take the second turn on the left, signposted 'Montefegatesi'. In
a short distance turn right, signposted 'Orridorio di Botri', soon
reaching the church at Bagni Caldi. Turn left along the side of
the church to the spacious parking area.

Refreshments: Bar at San Gemignano.

Map: Multigraphic, Garfagnana. Carta Territoriale, 1:50 000.

The Walk

Walk past the church, cross the road and go straight ahead along
the road opposite, signposted to the cemetery. Pass the cemetery
gate and continue along a narrow path, descending quite steeply.
In less than 100 metres, turn right, immediately before a concrete
slab bridge, downhill beside a little stream.

1. Turn left on reaching a minor surfaced road to walk high above
    the River Lima, the road soon diminishing to become a foot-
    path. Join another very minor road; turn right to cross a bridge
    over a stream then immediately turn left along a broad track
    heading for a house. Pass the house, keep right at a fork by a
    bamboo plantation, commencing the long ascent. Rake back
    to the left to follow the upper edge of the bamboo. A cobbled
    surface indicates the mule track origin of this route. The path
    weaves its way up the wooded hillside by a never-ending series
    of zig zags. Despite a little bramble the route is delightful, with
    views down to Bagni, but do spare a thought for the heavily
    laden mules! Suddenly the climb ends as we approach our first
    mountain village, Guzzano. Bear left to walk through the vil-
    lage, reaching tarmac close to the far end.

2. As the road forks, go right, slightly uphill; there is a chapel in
    the fork between roads. *The Apennine views are superb.* Climb

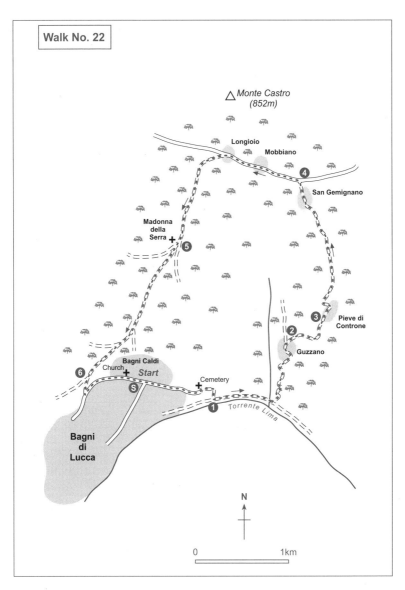

Walk No. 22

Monte Castro
(852m)

Longioio
Mobbiano

San Gemignano

Madonna
della
Serra

Pieve di
Controne

Guzzano

Bagni Caldi
Church   *Start*

Cemetery

Torrente Lima

Bagni
di
Lucca

N

0   1km

more steeply to pass an outlying part of the village. At a cobbled roadway turn right, uphill. As the track becomes
grass-grown, keep rising steadily, slanting across a hillside.
Pass a wayside cross, keeping right at a fork, up a mule track, to
pass a small building and enter Controne hamlet, now with
views up the valley of the River Lima.

3. Head for the church, passing to the right, then turn left behind the building. There is a blue 'footprint' waymark. Fork right in 10 metres, pass house no. 57, then turn right again, along a narrow path, gently downhill, soon passing old wash troughs set into the hillside. At an unsurfaced access road turn left to head down to San Gemignano, soon on tarmac, turning left to pass the church. Pass the bar, continuing to the end of the village. At the top of the village are a grocery shop and telephone box.

4. Cross the road to go straight ahead past the bus stop, rising a little on a rough surfaced roadway with an avenue of smallish trees on the left. *Monte Castro is impressive to the right.* Pass below a little cemetery, contouring round the hillside. At a fork as the hamlet of Mobbiano is approached, go left, descending gently between the houses. Leave the hamlet on a grass path, soon reaching tarmac. Turn left to continue. Reach Longioio, entering the village by its car park. Turn right at a 'T' junction in the village, steeply uphill, under an arch, bearing left to pass house number 29. At a fork in a few metres, follow a cobbled track descending to the left past house number 2.

    Keep left to pass isolated house number 3. Carry on along the unsurfaced road, above a house, keep left at a fork, slightly downhill, with former cultivation terraces on the right. The route winds through light woodland with occasional views back to the villages already visited and the mountain behind. Pass a water trough (not drinkable) and reach the lonely Chapel of Madonna della Serra.

5. Bear right, in front of the chapel, to follow the middle of the three facing tracks. Descend along the side of a wooded valley (there are, unusually, green and yellow arrows on some stones). *This is yet another former mule track.* Bagni di Lucca comes into view at the foot of the valley as the gradient becomes steeper. Ignore a left fork, pass a concrete waterworks building and, in less than 200 metres, as the track dips to the right, go straight ahead along a little path, steeply downhill for a short distance, to join an earth road. Turn left to pass a house and reach a hard surfaced road.

6. Fork left at once, downhill. The visible tower of Bagni Caldi church is useful as a destination point. Turn left along a road, still descending, to walk back to the church and parking area.

Places of interest

Although perhaps a little faded from its prime as a spa town, Bagni

Madonna della Serra chapel above Bagni di Lucca

di Lucca does retain a certain attraction for visitors. There is a long history of the use of thermal spring water for therapeutic purposes, from the middle ages to the present day, with an international reputation boosted by the presence of Europe's aristocracy over the years. Visits by several famous writers have helped in publicizing the virtues of the thermal baths. Just a touch of the former elegance remains.

The Ponte della Maddalena is a beautifully shaped high arched 12th-century bridge spanning the River Serchio, on the fringe of Borgo a Mozzano. The name of the bridge derives from a statue of Mary Magdalene, which stood close by. The bridge is also known as Ponte del Diavolo (Devil's Bridge). The statue is now in the parish church of San Iacopo, where there are also terracottas from the school of Andrea della Robbia.

Close to the south end of the Garfagnana, Bagni is well placed for visits to interesting places mentioned in walks 23, 24 and 25.

A few miles to the south, the historic city of Lucca has a great deal to offer to visitors. One of the oldest settlements in Tuscany, it stands on land drained by the Etruscans, soon becoming of both military and economic importance. The Romans built walls which were outgrown by the expansion of trade, prosperity and population in the Middle Ages, despite long running conflict with neighbouring Pisa. The city's independence was retained until 1799. The surrounding wall which is such a feature of present day Lucca was built in the 16th and 17th centuries. Inside the wall, the cathedral, the Pinacoteca Nationale, the Museo Nationale are all worth seeing. Those with musical interests should not miss the little museum at the birthplace of the composer Puccini, situated in a little piazza reached along the narrow Via del Possio, opposite the church of San Michele.

Other walks

Walks numbered 23 and 24 in this book. The more southerly routes included in the 'Hiking in Garfagnana' leaflet (see walk 25).

The locally produced 'Guide to Barga' has two suggested routes into the hills behind that town.

23. Trassilico

*In this short circuit based on the Apuan Alpine village of
Trassilico, most of the route is either steeply up or steeply
down, very much a sampler for more prolonged walking in
these mountains and a harder walk than the distance would
indicate. Unusually for Tuscany, the route is virtually all on
footpaths rather than cart tracks or forestry roadways. Some of
the paths are partially impeded by foliage in one or two places.
Plenty of woodland cover provides shade for hot days.*

Distance: 6km (3¾ miles). Total ascent: 1200ft (364m).

Start/car parking: Off-road spaces at entrance to Trassilico
village. To access Trassilico, take the minor road heading west
from Gallicano, which is in the Garfagnana valley bottom. In
less than 2 miles (3km) fork left for Verni to enjoy (except
perhaps, in the case of the driver) a slow scenic climb into the
mountain countryside, reaching Trassilico in 5 miles (8km).

Refreshments: Take your own.

Map: Multigraphic, Garfagnana, 1:50 000.

The Walk

Walk into the village. At the near end of a little piazza with a bust of
Luigi Pierotti, turn sharp left. There is a red and white waymark
and a 'Chieva' sign. Follow a track along the front of a large building and continue through chestnut woodland to the isolated
church of S. Ansana. After passing the church, turn right at once to
descend steadily on a broad track. Pass an old agricultural building. *The mountain scenery is spectacular.* Pass more old buildings
as the gradient increases, soon zig zagging down the steep hillside,
past a shrine/shelter, through oak woodland, with banks of primroses in very early spring. Chieva hamlet and a minor road come
into view below. At a 'T' junction turn right to reach farm buildings.

1. Turn right at a steeply ramped concrete roadway (waymark
    ahead) and carry on along a broad track, initially gravelled. Go
    straight ahead at a waymarked fork, ignore a track on the left
    and proceed to a waymarked stone building. Fork right, uphill,
    past a water trough and cross a valley. The path is now narrow
    but there is the occasional waymark. *Trassilico is in view on its
    hilltop ahead, the slope so steep that access from this side
    seems to be highly improbable.* Close to the head of another

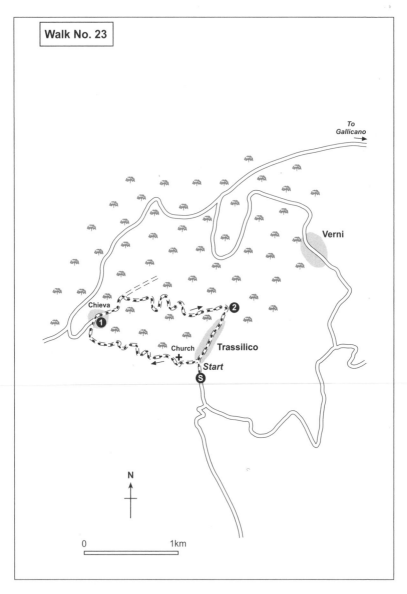

Walk No. 23

To
Gallicano

Verni

Chieva

❶

❷

Church

Trassilico

Start

S

N

0   1km

little valley, the path is eroded and part blocked by a fallen tree. Scramble across 2 small streams and continue, with some intrusive bramble. Serious ascent soon commences with innumerable zig zags up the hillside. At a 'T' junction turn left; there are former cultivation terraces to the right. Emerge quite suddenly into more open countryside, with views extending across the main Garfagnana valley to the distant Appennines.

Foothills of the Apuan Alps

At another 'T' junction turn left through a gap and bear to the right, then through another gap to join a more major path.

2. Turn right to walk into Trassilico, along a narrow street which runs the full length of the village, passing the church and the war memorial, before bearing left at the far end to return to the parking area.

Places of interest

Trassilico is a substantial ancient stone village perched defensively on a hilltop above the valley of the Turrite. Time has stood still here and dwellings remain close-packed, accessed by narrow streets, alleys and flights of steps.

A few miles further up the valley a major visitor attraction, the Grotta del Vento, offers underground tours of three different lengths throughout the year. In winter only the shortest (1 hour) visit is available, except at weekends.

Across the Garfagnana valley from Gallicano, the small town of Barga is regarded as the most attractive in the whole valley, combining a steeply graded walled medieval city with a modern town providing shops, hotels and other visitor facilities. The small cathedral is perched at the top of the medieval city, with a wonderful mountain backdrop.

To the south, the valley road leads to Lucca, a splendid old city of Etruscan and then Roman importance, with a broad topped surrounding wall providing a 2½-mile (4km) continuous promenade or cycle route. Cathedral, museums and churches provide much of interest for visitors. Music lovers should not miss the birthplace of Puccini in its little piazza with a bronze statue of the composer.

The house now has a little museum; it is found at the far end of the little Via de Possio, opposite the church of San Michele.

Other walks

Walks 22, 24 and 25 in this book and the others listed under walk 25.

24. Castelnuovo di Garfagnana

A short circular walk based on Castelnuovo di Garfagnana, the main town situated roughly half way along the extensive Garfagnana valley. The focal point of the walk is the huge fortress poised on the top of Monte Alfonso. Depending on the state of long-term works, it may or may not be possible to walk through the fortress. Some narrow, but perfectly good, footpath, otherwise broad forest track and some minor public road. There is a sustained but not too steep ascent through the forest. The route carries the name 'Sentiero dell Ariosto', commemorating a local poet of the 16th century.

Distance: 5km (3 miles). Total ascent: 800ft (242m).

Start/car parking: In Castelnuovo, towards the north end of town. Best is street-side parking close to the junction of the Via Garibaldi (main road from the north) and Via Azzi.

Refreshments: Plenty of choice in Castelnuovo.

Map: Multigraphic, Garfagnana, 1:50 000.

The Walk

From Via Garibaldi walk along Via Azzi. On the right, in 50 metres, is a board setting out the route of this circuit. Go up the steps beside the board and rise along a cobbled track, soon with rooftop views of the town. The path continues above outlying parts of the town, with the occasional red and white waymark. Go through a little gate to continue, a little up and down but generally following the contours, passing more outlying areas. The route is never in doubt. *To the left there are views of the ('marble') Apuan Alps.*

1. At the hamlet of Pasquigliora there are signposts for the 'Ariosto' footpath. Go to the right of a house, down steps, then straight on along a signposted track, now broad and stony, passing agricultural buildings. Bear to the right, below a hillside vineyard, pass a water supply building and ascend steadily through woodland. Go sharp right at a junction to continue up the side of Monte Alfonso; there are occasional red splodge waymarks. Near the top of the hill rake back sharp right at a junction to continue on the level before a last short ascent to the fortress, with its massive creeper-grown walls.

2. It might be possible to walk through the fortress via the obvious door. If not, turn left to follow a minor path along the foot of the walls. Continue to bear to the right, around the end of the

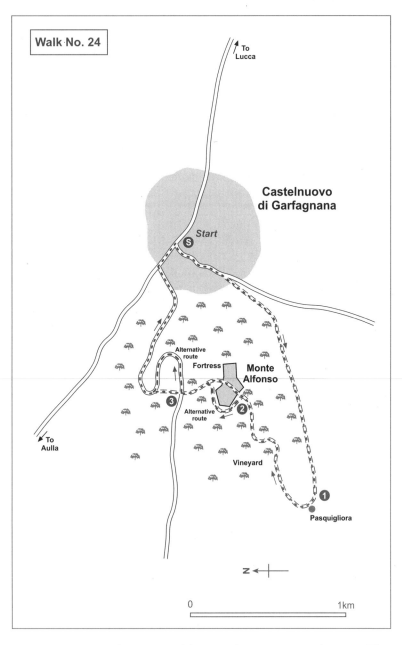

Walk·No. 24

To
Lucca

Castelnuovo
di Garfagnana

Start
Ⓢ

Alternative
route
Fortress

**Monte
Alfonso**

❸
Alternative
route

❷

To
Aulla

Vineyard

❶

Pasquigliora

z ←

0   1km

structure, passing an aerobic exercise course on the way. The main gate, facing Castelnuovo is eventually reached. Turn left to go down the fortress entrance roadway, as far as a surfaced public road.

3. Almost straight across the road is a former mule track, plunging down the rather overgrown hillside for a short distance to join a roadway. The roadway rejoins the surfaced road at a tight bend. *(Some walkers might prefer to walk beside the not very busy public road, by turning right at point 3, as the road descends towards Castelnuovo in a series of bends. The distance is about 800 metres).* In either case finish the walk by joining the main street opposite the Carabinieri, close to the Carlino hotel/restaurant and the recommended parking area.

Places of interest

Basically medieval, but with a more modern town superimposed, Castelnuovo has always looked more to the north towards Modena and Ferrara rather than to the more obvious Lucca and Florence for its historic political affiliations. As usual with the city states of northern Italy, there were centuries of spasmodic conflict, the town being defended by a great castle on a nearby hill; from origins in the 13th century, the castle was extended several times. The formidable outer walls are still almost intact.

See also walks 23 and 25 for other places of interest.

Other walks

Walks 23 and 25 in this book and the other suggested walks in those areas. The 'Garfagnana Trekking' route starts and finishes in Castelnuovo.

The 'Treno nel Parchi' leaflet/map (from tourist information) sets out routes in the Apuan Alps linked to stations on the railway line along the Serchio Valley

25. Vagli

A walk in the foothills of the Apuan Alps, those striking peaks streaked with gleaming marble. Vagli Sotto is a compact village on a knoll which forms a peninsula jutting into the artificial (but still very attractive) Lago di Vagli. Vagli Sopra is the sister village much higher up the side of the valley. In this circuit the two are connected by unsurfaced roadway, minor road and footpath, all good underfoot.

Distance: 7km (4½ miles). Total ascent: 450ft (136m).

Start/car parking: Car park by the entrance to Vagli Sotto village. From the main road in the Garfagnana valley, turn to the west at Poggio, about 5 miles (8km) north-west of Castelnuovo di Garfagnana and follow 'Vagli' signposts. Cross the lake by turning left at Pontile.

Refreshment: Café/bar at Pontile. Bar at Vagli Sopra.

Map: Multigraphic, Garfagnana, 1:50 000.

The Walk

Start down the Via Sotto access road, bending to the right at the bottom. *The staggering view of the nearby mountains is immediately apparent, with the differentiation of snow and marble quite difficult.*

1. At the junction by the bridge keep straight on. *There are occasional views of Vagli Sopra, perched on a shelf below the great bulk of Monte Roccandagia (1700m – 5579ft).* The traffic-free road soon loses its hard surface, climbing steadily at a modest gradient towards the superb peak of Monte Tambura (1890m – 6203ft). More height is gained via hairpin bends. The route heads for a disused quarry, with defunct buildings below.

2. Go sharp right below the buildings, then bear right at a road junction for an easy section to Vagli Sopra village, passing a small shrine.

3. Walk along the village street as far as a road junction, close to a bar. Turn right and, with the bar behind you, go down a steep cobbled alleyway with wide spaced steps. Turn right for 30 metres at the bottom (there is a green bar waymark on the ground). Before an old washing trough turn sharp left along a good grass path, descending gently behind the houses with views down the valley to the lake and Vagli Sotto. *Here, the*

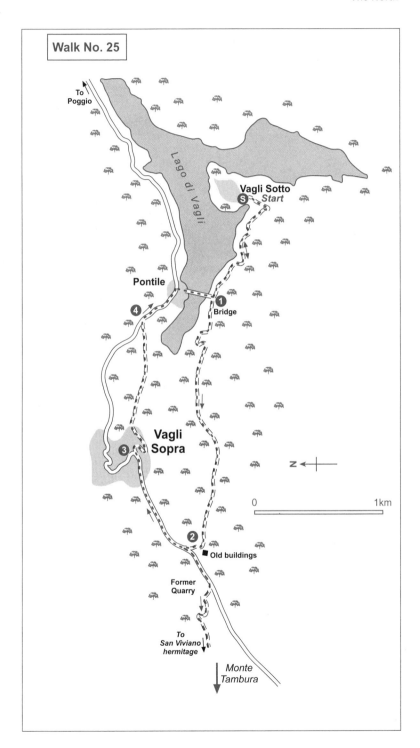

Walk No. 25

To Poggio

Lago di Vagli

Vagli Sotto
S Start

Pontile

4

1 Bridge

Vagli Sopra

3

N

0   1km

2
■ Old buildings

Former Quarry

To San Viviano hermitage

Monte Tambura

Vagli Sotto

wild crocuses are in flower as early as mid February. Pass a dilapidated old building and, as the track swings to the left, take the footpath on the right, descending more steeply. Join a tiny road, turning right but soon forking left to follow a path below a house on the right (sign 'Vagli Sotto'). A grass track continues the descent, passing a red and white waymark on a post; the bridge is soon in view. The path is not always entirely clear, but is helped by the occasional waymark. Join a little road by a sports area, turning left. Cross a stream and rise past a school to join a more important road.

4.   Turn right to walk downhill to Pontile. Turn right to the bridge, crossing to reach point 1 of the outward route. Turn left to return to Vagli Sotto.

Places of interest

With the little town of Castelnuovo di Garfagnana as its focal point, the whole of the long valley of the River Serchio, known as the Garfagnana, forms a most attractive division between the mountains of the Apuan Alps to the west and those of the Appennines to the east. In the mountain foothills tiny old villages perch improbably in apparently inaccessible locations. To the north the Parco dell Orecchiella covers a large area (52 sq. km.) of protected countryside at high level in the Appennines, with a visitor centre (open in season).

The Casa Abrami at Vagli Sotto is an exhibition centre with a display including themes of mountains, water and energy in addition to local archaeological finds.

North-east of Castiglione di Garfagnana is the Museo Don Luigi Pellegrini, featuring a collection of local items, including costumes and craftwork. Open all the year round.

Other walks

Extend this walk from Vagli di Sopra to the Hermitage of San Viviano, via Campocatina (about 3 hours of quite hard walking there and back).

Walks 23 and 24 in this book.

Garfagnana trekking route – nine stages of mountain trekking, leaflet 'Hiking in Garfagnana' (in English) from tourist information. Several shorter walks suggested in the same leaflet.

In the same series:

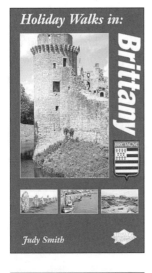

Holiday walks in	
BRITTANY	**£9.95**
DORDOGNE	**£8.95**
LOIRE VALLEY	**£9.95**
NORMANDY	**£9.95**
COSTA DEL SOL	**£8.95**
ALPUJARRA	**£9.95**
MALLORCA	**£9.95**